Visitations

Daily Contacts From His Heart to Ours

Volume 1

Messages received by

Miriam Grosjean

Our Lady of Light Publications
P.O. Box 17541
Ft. Mitchell, KY 41017

In conformity with the decrees of Pope Urban VIII, the Publisher recognizes and accepts that the final authority regarding these messages rests with the Holy See of Rome, to whose judgment we willingly submit.

The decree of the Congregation for the Propagation of the Faith A.A.S. 58, 1186 (approved by Pope Paul VI on October 14, 1966) states that the Imprimatur is no longer required on publications that deal with new revelations, apparitions, prophesies or miracles, provided that they contain nothing contrary to faith and morals.

—The Publisher

This book is published by Our Lady of Light Publications, a subsidiary of Our Lady of Light Foundation, a tax exempt corporation. Our Lady of Light Foundation is a religious public charitable Gospa ministry association organized to foster support for Our Lady of Light Ministries and Our Lady of the Holy Spirit Center.

For additional copies, write to:
Our Lady of Light Publications
P.O. Box 17541
Fort Mitchell, KY 41017

Library of Congress Catalog Card No.: 87-50461

ISBN: 0-9635-852-4-X

 First OLLP Printing: February, 1994

About the cover picture:
This famous line drawing depicts Our Lord as a visitor knocking at the door, asking for entry. Not usually noticed at first glance is the fact that the door has no outdoor latch and thus can only be opened by the owner—*from the inside*. Our Lord visits us all but only enters where the owner opens the door to Him. To each who opens the door He gives the gift of His kingdom.

Our Lord's Forward

People in these latter days need to be informed how to live. They must also know of My goodness and mercy.

My anointing has been given to My workers possessing My gifts. They are obligated to get My words out to the best of their abilities.

Authors through the ages have been given inspiration from above, dating back to the time when the Bible was written. Those who have fed upon My words have been blessed. Their faith has grown in unlimited proportions. My spiritual writers of the present age have been enlightened by the Holy Spirit to pass information on to My starving people who suffer from lack of knowledge.

Readers should pray for discernment. They will thus be able to separate truth from error. I speak through My righteous people to open their spiritual eyes to see and ears to hear. No one is forced to believe for I let their wills have complete reign. But those who seek will find. My people are not left orphans.

It is My wish for none to perish. Just as the body needs food to live, so, too, the soul needs spiritual food to digest daily. The Eucharist was instituted by Me to feed all of My people. Those who celebrate at My table receive the light of life. Be cognizant of My props and your life can be lived to the fullest.

Author's Preface

In the stillness of the early morning hours, upon awakening, I have written down inspired sentences as dictated to my mind by the Holy Spirit. I promised the Lord on January 1, 1985 that I would publish a book if given messages daily. The writings in this book represent the fulfillment of that promise.

Since this first book was printed, three other volumes of *Visitations* have followed. I became my own publisher and have had the books printed on a limited basis. Comments I have received from the readers have been astounding. Mainly, these readers have related how much the messages have helped to increase their faith, how they became aware of the Trinity's presence and how their problems have been relieved by their putting into practice the truths presented in these books.

Through the Lord's urgings to give the books to a publisher with wide distribution, I started saying the 54 day Rosary Novena so that I might be led to the right person.Our Lady of Light Publications called during the second day of my novena. OLLP has now published one of my (the Lord's) books, *His Power*, and several more books are planned for the near future. You are invited to read for yourself with an open mind the following daily messages to arrive at your own opinion.

Our Lord has dictated four volumes of "Visitations" to me (daily messages during four consecutive years). These were followed by *His Power* and then books entitled *Fruits of the Spirit* and *Gifts of the Spirit*, a supplement to *Fruits of the Holy Spirit*. Most recently I have been working on messages addressing God's *Charismatic Gifts*. His work continues.

Note From the Editor

A book like Visitations evokes some common reader reactions. The first is a fascination that God might visit some lowly human to pass on comments for a larger audience. Then there is curiosity about the receiver's personality and how that individual came to be chosen for such a mission. Finally there comes a point where the reader feels drawn, by the messages alone, to a higher plane of appreciation for God and closer, ever closer, to Him, the source of life and love. The lessons herein do not therefore so much depend on the size, shape or disposition of the original receiver as on the attitude of the reader to use the messages as a vehicle for growing more in God. We are, after all, placed on this earth to make the best we can of ourselves and our fellows and, in the end, to grow to love God to the best of our ability. Words by Him are only reinforcement in our struggle upward.

The messages in this book should serve to increase our knowledge of God and our awareness of His constant presence. But that is just the beginning. As Rev. William G. Most said in his book, *Mary in Our Life,*[1] "The more one knows, the more he *ought* to love God, the more *motives* he has at his disposal which should urge him on to love." (Italics are the original author's.) This book, then, provides the reader with knowledge, yes, but, more importantly, with a vehicle for building a fresh new spiritual appreciation for Him, a renewed resolve to grow closer to Him because it just makes sense. And can there be a better vehicle source than God's own words?

Categorizing messages alleged to be from heaven can be a difficult task—for several reasons. First of all, no absolute standards of classification for such messages exist. Secondly, messages to "listeners" are received in diverse ways. Thirdly, messages are inevitably reported from the mind of and through the faculties of the receiver. Phenomena like the receipt of messages are classified by some as "extraordinary mystical phenomena." These, in turn, can be further divided into two broad categories, one called "private revelations" and the other called "charisms" (the gifts of the Holy Spirit).[2] Further classifications and distinctions are made as one progresses deeper and deeper into mystical theology but, suffice it to say for present purposes, caution must always be exercised regarding the hearing of words of seemingly divine origin, for the source is not always divine. Great care must be exercised in the discerning of such phenomena. Eventually it comes down to trusting in God to care for us as we walk in good faith and praying to Him for the gift of prudent judgment.

The editors of this book attest that the messages herein have been thoroughly reviewed for doctrinal congruity. We believe them to be well within the realm of Catholic Church teaching. We cannot stipulate the exact nature of the source of the words as written other than to say that the words, the witness and the circumstances show multiple signs that the messages themselves are divinely sourced.

The following pages consist of what might be called "direct, intellectual, supernatural words," or simply "promptings," a term allowing more personal phraseology on the part of the receiver. In any event, these messages are enthusiastically presented as having admirable spiritual merit. We welcome the reader to a warm spiritual adventure.

— Larry Memering, Editor
Our Lady of Light Publications

---

[1] Rev. William G. Most, *Mary in Our Life,* Doubleday, New York, 1963, page 15.

[2] Very Rev. Adolphe Tanquerey, *The Spiritual Life, A Treatise on Ascetical and Mystical Theology,* Desclée & Company, Tournai, Belgium, 1930, page 702.

JANUARY

January 1

My heart longs for your company. I patiently wait for your companionship. Discuss your problems with Me, even the smallest, for I have an attentive ear. I can put your mind at ease, but oftentimes asking your neighbor for advice only leads to confusion. Be loving, kind and humble in all your transactions with My people. They will then be drawn to you like a magnet. Spread My love to all those I send to you. Joy will permeate your being while you are pleasing Me. You will be walking to My heavenly beat and we can keep perfect pace together.

January 2

The paths of My followers are illuminated by My light. The dark clouds will not hinder My righteous from the goals I have set for them. These goals cannot be accomplished by their own might, but I will establish the power necessary to reach them. This power makes all things possible. Your service for Me is inspired, sending you to heights unknown. My hand is not shortened. Reach out to Me and I will reach out to you. This contact is a spiritual encounter that lifts your spirit high and brings excitement in your so-called dull life. This is My menu for you to keep on top of your world.

January 3

My followers will not be lonely.. My word will be in their hearts and on their lips. The more they ask, the more they will receive. The more they seek the more they will find. Sit silently saying My name, Jesus, and you will feel Me, oh, so near. Then listen and I will tune you into the spiritual world. Apply no effort on your part. Fit quiet times into your busy schedule and you will be renewed in both mind and spirit. I need you to help carry on My work in the earth. You have no idea of your tremendous potential when you commit yourself over to Me entirely. This is the commitment I wait for patiently. Partial commitments will not do. I need and want all of you. You can then anticipate great rewards in this world and the world to come.

January 4

Marvel at the beauty around about you, all made by My word. Righteousness will be rewarded beyond your imagination. The human mind cannot fathom the great riches I have in store for My faithful people. Your struggles will not be in vain. My word does not say your life will be easy but it does promise reward. Some of you have to wait until the next life but you can still find peace in your turbulent world. My word does not come back to Me void. All that is promised is for each and every one. There are no exceptions. So run your race in life to win and take others with you. Speak with your lips My wonders and watch how they come to pass. I will never forsake anyone who calls upon Me. My way for them may not be what they ask but will lead them to My Throne Room.

January 5

Rest in My love. Drink in My presence. I am your God that healeth you. Your strength is restored in your quiet time with Me. Just you in Me and I in you — a one relationship. I wish to reveal My face to you. You can see Me now through your spiritual eyes — little short glimpses in the beginning but more as time goes on. Our longing to be together is true love taking form. My grace is being poured into you, as I want you to have more of My gift. Time will enhance our love affair.

January 6

Happy are My people who meditate on My life. They become aware of My values. Wisdom becomes a part of them. They do not need the riches of life to be content. Their ecstasy is knowing Me. The more they read My word, the more they want to do My will. The self life disappears as they reach out to My people. Life becomes interesting and meaningful. Their time is used wisely and not wasted. I open My followers' eyes to see all this through My light. You are beginning to comprehend some of My principles. Much more will be opened to you. Keep listening, My beloved, for revelations I will reveal to you. We will share so much together. Just relax and wait on Me and I will not disappoint you. If My people only knew My longing for their intimate conversation, they would respond. Tell them as often as you can. You will be sowing the seed and I will water it. Together we can accomplish more then you could imagine.

January 7

Visit the shut-ins and the lonely. Worry not what to say. I will put the words in your mouth. My people need to know that I have not forsaken them. They can call on Me. You can bring My peace to them. Anything you do for them you receive back in return. My workers are not losers but only gainers. My love will be poured out to you to be poured into others. The busier you are doing My work, the happier you will become. Once you experience this, you will rejoice. Yes, My dear, rejoice in Me always. Never stop praising My name.

January 8

Press onward with courage, My child, knowing that victory lies ahead. You are rich in My grace and sustaining power. Keep your eyes on your eternal goal and keep following the straight and narrow way. My people need a pattern to follow so let your light be seen. Work among them as an apostle, humbly showing the way either by action or a few words of love. Kindness will always go a long way in winning people over to Me. If each of My disciples do a little part, I can take over with My power. Together we can be a team in bringing people to My Kingdom.

January 9

My daughter, reach out to others and share the knowledge you have of the spiritual realm. These people, in turn, can share with others and thus take on a snowball effect. My people must learn to keep in the spirit to enable them to survive. Worldly things will cease to bother you. You can live in My joy amidst the turmoil. Blissful sleep will be yours for your mind has learned to be quiet. Bodily functions can continue in the perfect rhythm set at creation. Disease and sickness cannot attack such a body. My people have great compensations but unfortunately few realize My way of life for them.

January 10

Prayer is the key to unlock the door to spirituality. It taps into the power on high and is never left unanswered. It works for good for the recipient of our prayer. It may not be answered in the way your prayer was directed but remember the soul is more important than the body. Life is so short compared to eternity. I honor prayer in ways you do not dream possible. Do not give up or think I am not listening. Your prayers work in a two-fold way — for the good of the person's soul and for the improved strength of your own soul, giving you grace abounding. Never stop praying but press on to your high calling.

January 11

Release all your burdens and bodily ills to Me. Then think not on them but, with all the strength you have, pray for all My people. It is the releasing of self-life that you enter the real life. This life brings a gradual healing for self. As you feel this new strength seeping in, branch out to others. Keep your mind busy but off of everything pertaining to self. Read My word, meditating on it day and night. My grace and power can lift you out of despair. Your new way of life will be felt by those around you. The evil forces try to hold you down but you can break loose from these bonds. Asking for My help will send My heavenly forces to your rescue. Believe and you will receive. Practice this, ridding your mind of all negative thoughts and replacing them with positive thoughts. It is not easy to change, so continue asking for My help. Life is not easy but, lived out My way, lifts the burden and earns for you a high place in My Kingdom.

January 12

Your thoughts are so important to your well being. Never dwell on anything that is not good and pure. Hold no bitter thoughts toward anyone. Erase them. If you will abide by this, your face will take on a beautiful countenance. Sing, laugh and be happy in spite of adverse conditions. A merry heart pleases Me and I am always ready to pour out My grace and blessings on such a one. This merriment can be infectious to those around and oftentimes swings their mood upward. Many an argument in a household can be averted when happiness abounds. Oh, if only people would use My keys to a happy, contented life — all found in My word.

January 13

I have given My spirit to each and every true believer. He will guide you in truth and righteousness. Listen to that inner voice and you will receive heart knowledge, not head knowledge. You must learn to differentiate between the two. I promised My apostles I would send them a comforter, the Holy Spirit. This was fulfilled and has been given to all My righteous, believing people through to the present age. Speak to the Holy Spirit. Acknowledge Him from within and He will direct your paths. This is My very special gift to you. This is My great love offering to all My people. They are never alone but always have the indwelling of the Holy Spirit.

January 14

My grace will take you through every heartache, every disappointment, every illness and every emotional crisis. You are being molded for greater positions in My Kingdom. If this truth would only sink into your subconsciousness, you could go about undisturbed by any attack from the evil one. In these fiery assaults, My children are being molded into My image. During attacks keep your mind on My Son's passion but never on the "poor me" attitude. This lesson that I am trying to convey will bring you out of each situation quickly and not put upon you diseases that anxiety and worry cause. The world is in a difficult period but it need not be difficult for My people. Always be open for change keeping in mind My tremendous outpouring of My power and grace.

January 15

Do not let your broken lives and shattered dreams keep you down in spirit. You have a beautiful mansion waiting for you in the sky. My world which is the one you pass on to has streets of gold. Everything is more beautiful than the human eye could possibly see in your world. The human mind is not able to comprehend the vast magnitude of My universe with its majestic music to please the ears and its vivid colors to please the eyes. You may marvel at times at the nature in your world. This is all well and good because I created it by My word but wait until you see the grandeur of nature in your world to come. My righteous should never fear death. Their death will be only swallowed up in victory.

January 16

Reach out to others and I will reach out to you. Your instantaneous help will touch their lives. They will want to pattern their lives with gifts you possess. Example will lead more people to Me than preaching and teaching. My light will shine through you best by the deeds you do for others in a demure manner, taking no credit for yourself but only knowing I am working through you. Working for Me is not drudgery, as I lift the load, making it lighter. Relaxing in this knowledge makes it possible for you to accomplish My work in your world. You automatically become a servant of the Lord, earning for yourself a high position in your world.

January 17

Give and keep giving and I will see that your supply never runs out. To whom much has been given, much will be required. Substantiate your gifts from above with your generosity. A happy disposition will develop and spread to your counterparts. Back up the good deeds with continual prayer. This encases you in the spirit and the enemy has no entrance. Your joy will increase rapidly and you will be blessed with continual health and energy. Try Me and see if the gates of Heaven are not opened unto you.

January 18

Don't ever stop praying. Keep our communication line open. The prayers of My righteous are heard and answered — answered for the good of the person's well being related to eternal life. Too many of My people become indignant toward Me when they think their prayers are not being answered. This shows their lack of trust toward Me. With the right attitude while praying and the knowing that I am listening, your prayers will always be acknowledged. I take into consideration the betterment of the soul. The souls that I want close to Me often endure hardship to earn that closeness. They, in time, begin realizing this and thank Me for their trials. Life takes courage and a determination to do My will. How happy people become when their eyes are open to see My way rather than theirs. To reach this point requires continual prayers. Prayer, in due time, can become a beautiful ritual.

January 19

Thoughts are so important to your well being. Keep them under control at all times. Your thoughts pretty much determine your destiny. You have the power to control your thoughts given to you by My grace. Bad thoughts, worry, anxiety, etc. may creep into your subconscious by means of the evil one, but the power I have given you should take over immediately and erase these thoughts. You alone have the free will to entertain these thoughts or cast them out. Calling on Me for help, followed by prayer and meditation, will always see you through. Remember My grace is sufficient. The more you practice, the sooner the devil will flee and the happier you will become. As long as you entertain any thoughts that can lead you astray, the evil one will stick around. You may say, "I can't", but practice is the answer. My saints all followed this method and you, too, can be lead to sainthood.

January 20

By My passion and resurrection I have set you free. Walk in this freedom and pass it on to others. Dwell on My passion and you will experience the love I have for all My people. Never look at their shortcomings but only their potential in My spirit world. None of My people are perfect but they are all working toward perfection. I will honor this and help mold them into My image. It may be a slow, gradual process with ups and downs, but the more you apply My principles, the quicker you will succeed in your growth toward holiness. Cherish every step of your spiritual life and long to be in My will. That inner void can only be satisfied when you render yourself to Me wholeheartedly.

January 21

As you grow in grace you can begin calling on Me for strength and courage to perform certain tasks. You will become amazed at the outcome for My power is given to My faithful followers to show My strength in their weakness. This is why your Christian life becomes exciting. I answer your calls and come to your rescue. The key is to remain humble and know I am working through you and with you. You will be endowed with a calm assurance that, whatever the task, it will be accomplished in a super manner. Why? Because you have learned to experience My power. In the natural you have your limitations but in the supernatural there are no limitations. As My children continue to grow in grace they will begin feeling some reactions to the lesson I am conveying to you.

January 22

You are bone of My bone and flesh of My flesh for I am in you. Life takes on a new meaning when this principle is understood deep in your spirit. You yearn more and more to do My work among My people. You shall grow more like Me in thought, word and action. Your fellow believers will discern this quality in you. Your straightforward answers will be satisfying to the hungry souls seeking Me. Your prayer life will automatically increase. No life formed against you will prosper. This is why I tell you that you are rich beyond measure.

January 23

When I am made Lord of your life, I bring you peace in the midst of your trials. I do not work in the people who do not invite Me into their heart. When I am invited, I work with those people and send the Holy Spirit to dwell within them and instruct and guide them. Their decisions are My decisions for their lives. If My people would only realize this, they could relax no matter the outcome. Life would no longer be a battle. The sting of hardship would be removed. I would begin replacing their stoney heart with a loving heart which would eventually reach out to My people. Love would become so instilled in them that they would want to pass it on to others. Such action pleases Me beyond measure. My people's trust is exemplified in the handling of their affairs. My blessing is always upon them.

January 24

Fix your eyes on the 'heavenlies.' You are running your race on earth for your heavenly reward. Each day you press on toward your high calling. Whatever happens is My will. If your day does not seem to go right, it is only because self enters. Otherwise you would take your trials in stride. Many hardships endured for Me means greater reward at the finish line. Do not let anything or anyone, including your thoughts, rob you of your prize. This knowledge ingrown in your spirit will make your world grow dim and nothing will bother you. I give you the strength to take you through each day. So, my child, keep pressing onward and upward.

January 25

Be still and know that I am your God, ever present with you. I work along with you when you call upon Me, giving you strength and courage for sustenance. Those who do not call on Me often make the wrong turns and are not backed by My spiritual support. The evil one will try to squeeze in wherever he can. The more you get into the practice of praying, the more you will automatically call on Me for help. I love My righteous people and know what is most important for their well-being. This is why I sent My Son to earth. His sufferings have freed all My people who believe and ask His forgiveness. Spread this word quickly for time is running out. I do not want My people to perish. Speak up and be bold for My Son's sake. He will not have suffered and died in vain if My elected followers would harken to My prompting and heed their calling. My Son stands between your world and eternity. One must go through Him, the eternal Judge. Call on His name often for whatsoever your plea.

January 26

Never cease to worship and praise Me. I am listening and ready to administer to your needs. The needs vary in all My people. Supplying them is not always in their best interest. I see beyond their capabilities. I know the needs of souls but they are unknown to people on their own part. This is why thanking and praising for every happening, no matter what, brings sweet music to My ears and echoes throughout the heavens. A thankful heart becomes a joyful heart. A trust ensues which is beneficial beyond a person's comprehension. My storehouse gets fuller and fuller for each individual following My word for his or her way of life.

January 27

Be still and know that I am God. I visit people in the stillness. I wait until they are resting in the spirit. Then they become an open channel to flow through. Often My living waters are flowing through them, cleansing them and restoring their strength. Anyone calling on My spirit receives an infilling of some sort. I do not leave My people unaided. Often I build a small fire of love within and fan it now and then to spread throughout their whole being. Or I plant a seed of faith and fertilize it now and then watching the faith grow. I wish more of My people would ask for My gifts and then believe when they receive them. Freely I give to all who call upon My name.

January 28

My heart aches for all My people. They do not apply My way for abundant living. They run to and fro trying to please everyone. Their way of life and mine are different. If they would apply My word, they would learn a more systematic approach to all their dilemmas. They would have energy left over for My work. Your top priority is to please Me. Others will get served in the proportionate measure of My will. Asking Me to take over your life puts Me in control and your burden becomes lighter. I can then mold you into My image. You will begin seeing with your spiritual eyes your potential in serving Me in the spiritual realm. Life in your world has little meaning of itself, but served out for Me in obedience to My word, it becomes meaningful and exciting and you will have the great eternal reward of sublime bliss for ever and ever.

January 29

The complexities of life are often brought about by rebellion to My complete way of life for your well-being. If My followers do not receive their petitions, it is because My granting such would be for the harm of your soul or the souls of those involved. Bearing your cross patiently, in complete submission to My will, casts upon you great honor from above and is all recorded in My book of life. Your loved ones did not suffer and die in vain. If you could only see the aesthetic state they are experiencing, you would shout for joy. Since you cannot see them with your natural eyes, try to picture them with your spiritual eyes of faith. This will keep you content until the homecoming.

January 30

Fear must be cast out as soon as it enters your mind. It was planted there by the evil one. Often fear creeps in during an illness. Remember I said the devil comes to steal, to kill and to destroy. I came that you might have life. Trusting Me can bring about that life. Your health can return in short order. But entertaining the promptings of the devil can keep you sick from the fear it imparts. Practice forcing fear out of your mind. Entertain healthy thoughts, profess them, and they shall come into being. Pass this information on to your counterparts for the devil is in his final sprints in these last days.

January 31

The criticality of the nations has about reached its peak. The very foundation of the earth is being shaken but still My people live as though there is no tomorrow. Gratification of the flesh is their number one aim in life. My anger has poured out wrath upon them but they are blind to the signs. Woe to those who do not turn to Me in repentance. My patience has about run out. Some have listened and their protection will be sealed. That some are even dying for their faith should open the eyes of the nations. Still blindness is prevalent. Much prayer needs to be rendered to make an about turn. My Son died to save all people paying the price for their freedom, yet the ears stay closed and there is the refusal to accept this truth. The consequence will be too horrendous to describe. My handful of evangelists are getting the word out but they are being laughed at. Woe to those who reject the warnings, but happy are those who heed them.

FEBRUARY

February 1

Your heart and mine can be fused as one. Our secret rendezvous become more numerous as time passes. Loving My people will become a daily pastime and bring to you joy unspeakable and My glory to the fullest. You are being lifted. You feel it in your step while walking, being raised higher, toward a place in your eternal home. My children's callings are varied and yours is a unique one. Living day by day in our anticipated visits is what you were created to do. Man's sin separated us but your growing knowledge and practice of My word has rekindled our love relationship. This in-depth growth must be ingrained in My followers so that coping with everyday problems can become less burdensome. As our love constantly deepens, so will your love for your fellow men. This is the epitome of love being carried to heights unknown.

February 2

My people should not allow stagnation to enter into their life. No matter the age, they should keep growing spiritually. My word has a lifetime of study in it. The deeper you dig the more it becomes alive to you. This keeps you alive and I bless you with a keen intellect to comprehend the spiritual intonation. Do not expect wonders for I release My powers into you gradually according to what each individual can take. Each person's prayer life must develop along with a giving of the gifts which have been bestowed on that person. All this can be worked into a busy schedule by the sorting out of priorities. You can be energized by your want and thirst for the truth. I do not ask that you burn the night oils for rest is vital to the body. You must not neglect your work in life, nor steal from an employer. Time left over is yours to use wisely but never the time for the duties of your state in life. My followers can accomplish much with careful planning and prayed for help from above. Remember that with Me all things are possible.

February 3

Be diligent in all your ways. Conformity should be your life-style — striving earnestly to do My will. Seek the good things in life for entertainment so you can keep holy as I am holy. See Me in others and, if you discern otherwise, lift that person up in prayer. Never judge, for often there are reasons unknown to you for someone's action. Be a friend to those you encounter, always willing to lend a hand. Be on guard for you may be instrumental in the beginning stages of that person's salvation. I work in unusual ways and often plant My people where they are needed if only for a smile to pick someone up or maybe for a prayer needed in their behalf. Lending an ear is often just what someone needs. The repercussion of helping someone always benefits you. This is the way My law works so do not cease doing good works among My people. Be on guard that evil forces are constantly at work and will especially creep into your thoughts. Changing your thoughts immediately by prayer and meditation will drive them out. Pray until you feel My love taking over and enveloping your whole being.

February 4

Unleash the shackles that bind you. You have this power. Your anointing is from above, so exercise your authority. Your spirit-man can rise up from within and conquer things you never dreamed possible. This strength is felt by your whole being giving you assurance of the task at hand. The accomplishment of the task will delight, excite and surprise you. A joy will ensue that will bring about much glory and you can keep going from glory to glory. This newfound glory will be almost too wonderful to behold. At times you will feel like you are floating on air. Next, it is back to reality, knowing that these glorious moments will have reoccurrence. Your prayer life will keep these moments precious to you. You will be living in your world on a higher plane. Your humble attitude will remain, however, since you know your own power could not do what Our power can do. Keep praising, for the glory of the Lord has come and is upon you.

February 5

Immerse yourself in My love. It will form a shield of protection around you. I love everyone so much and want each to join our heavenly staff. This position must be earned in your world. If you obey My statutes and make an earnest effort toward that goal, I will stay with you constantly nudging you on. Do not allow your troubles to weigh you down. They are your means of salvation, depending upon how you handle them. The greater the troubles, the greater are the rewards, if carried out by the rules laid down in My word. You have the sword of the spirit which is My word to fight off attacks from Satan. The more scripture you quote, the more weapons you have at your disposal. The same can be said for prayer. Worry and anxiety are lifted when My laws are applied and adhered to. Once you discover the truth of what I am saying, you are set free. You then should try to relate this truth to your friends, loved ones, and even strangers, so they too can be set free. You will not only be doing them a favor but I will find favor in you and will pour out more grace and blessings upon you.

February 6

Be of one heart and one mind with love as your theme. Love conquers all pursuits in life. It binds up the wounds of the brokenhearted. It frees the captives. It reaches out to all with outstretched arms filling them with the quality which leads to My Kingdom. My Son was sent for your true example. Pattern your life after Him. Seek the good things in life and they will be yours. I fulfill My promises. Love never fails.

Strive for it and you will be a winner in your life as well as the next. My people will be gainers for having known such a person possessing this highest of qualities—love.

February 7

In the measure you give, it will be given back to you in overflowing amounts. To those that are given much, much is expected in return. All gifts from above are to be shared. If not, misery creeps in and destroys what you do have. My people have a tendency to store up for the future. But only in your heavenly home are your rewards stored up for you and counted by your good deeds. Every act of kindness is remunerated on your day of judgment. Your whole life will be opened up before you in a quick flash. Nothing will be added or taken away from your record. If My people would only open their spiritual eyes and see what is about to occur, they would mend their ways. Begin laying up for yourselves the things that count toward your eternal inheritance. Give away what you cannot use so others can benefit from your excess. This action will keep My blessings flowing your way.

February 8

Be ever ready to serve Me. The harvest is ripe and my workers are few. Fear not to speak out in My name. Soak up My words so that My words can be on your lips for others. This way you will be imitating Me. Let your light shine and be a beacon to draw others to you. Saving a soul is one of the highest accomplishments in My service. Pray for guidance and you will obtain it. When you offer your time and service to Me, I will utilize them, placing certain people in your path. Your spirit will begin to recognize My promptings. Oftentimes just a few words can be seeds to plant to start the growth of faith in others. Keep yourself in prayer so the enemy will not hinder your good work. Pray for the ones you are helping and do not give discouragement entrance. Then trust Me for I work along side you. Never doubt My presence.

February 9

There may be times that you feel you are going through raging waters but if you are in My will, obeying My statutes, you are being washed in the living waters, often preparing you for greater works. When the waters become calm, you have reached a new era in your life. You may find that you have a greater urge to minister to My people. Your values in life have changed. Then keep looking to Me for guidance. Keep in prayer for often My plans for your life are different than what you may have in mind. Mine may seem impossible to you but follow My lead and the grace I give you makes it possible. You can't do without Me and I need you to carry on My work, that of saving souls for My Kingdom. You may not see it as yet but, when you do, you will experience a joy that will carry you through the turbulent waters that occur from time to time in each one's life.

February 10

The more you believe in Me and meditate on My word, the more I will reveal Myself to you. One must first have a pure heart with malice toward no one. Increasing your prayer life, coupled with meditation and praise, brings alive My spirit to you. You then experience an ecstasy that nothing on the human plane can exceed. It is at this stage when My revelations are most prevalent. Being alone with no distractions keeps you in this state longer. The quiet Heavenly atmosphere creates little healings in the body, for My power can work when your whole being is in this state. Ask and you shall receive but only if it is for the good of your soul or the soul of the person for whom your petition is made. Always, in some way, you will be aided spiritually. Never stop looking up with expectancy.

February 11

Draw nigh unto Me and I will draw nigh unto you. Our relationship can grow more dear as time passes on. Your complete trust in Me will bring about a satisfaction that money cannot buy. Contentment, no matter the circumstances, will be yours to enjoy. You will not mind the aging process for you have learned that I am All in All. Death will not be something dreaded but a journey to look forward to with anticipated excitement. When My righteous do cross over, they receive a welcome they cannot possibly fathom. My righteous will see the great rewards they earned for following Me. In spite of their struggles and conflicts, they did not turn Me aside but kept right on going toward their eternal goal. They will be greeted with My favorite phrase, "Well done, My good and faithful servant."

February 12

I will come quickly so be prepared. Tell others to do likewise. I infuse in My followers a good measure of love. This love is to be used to win over the people headed in the wrong direction. It can heal the brokenhearted and bind up the wounds. Love can melt the hardest of hearts. My people are reaching out for it. You who have obtained it, give it out freely. The perfect giver of love was My Son. Dwell on His life often, especially His passion. Love your enemies and the unlovely. This can come about by praying for them. Shoot prayers to Me often through the day instead of pondering on self. This can become a habit and you will not be left unrewarded. Blessed are My prayers for they shall become My warriors and, in turn, conquerors.

February 13

Train up children in the way they should go. Parents have a duty to see that their children hear the right words. Characters are formed early in life. Time should be given unselfishly to mold them. The home that has My peace is the ideal one. If children stray after you have performed your duties, do not fret. Each has been given his or her own free will. When that child comes of age, you are released of your duties but never stop praying for that child. The complexities in life are varied. Trials and hardships are often too numerous to understand. Unless you seek Me, you shall fall. My grace, when in My will, will carry you through all your valleys. Persevere, my beloved ones, until we meet face to face. It will be worth it all.

February 14

Be attentive to the needs of the poor. You who have been blessed with earthly gifts should reach out and share with those less fortunate. For, to those that are given much, much is required. If you have little in material possessions, a helpful hand will be indeed blessed. Every action on your part is written down in the Lamb's Book of Life. Prayers offered up for the poor and needy are another act of charity. If My people only knew My counting system, they would cease wasting time and spend it on doing good. You will be laying up for yourselves blessings untold. Be not vexed at your neighbor's prosperity for earthly gain is fleeting. Strive for your Heavenly calling that lasts forever.

February 15

Seek My peace and you will have it. My peace will keep you calm in all the storms of life. Disease cannot take a hold on a body in this tranquil state. A person that can stay content knowing I am in charge will be able to encounter this peace. My righteous can reach this sublime state if they realize that all things happen for good to those that love Me. I intervene to make things right for your well being. Patience added to this peace can bring you through trying times. In later years you will be able to comprehend My workings in your life. The peace I give cannot be given by your world. It is a gift I give to My children who obey My laws and work at doing My will. Pray and ask for this peace and I will not withhold this gift from you. Keep in your remembrance that all good and perfect gifts come from above.

February 16

Use My Son's name often. It has healing properties. Recited in time of trouble, it brings instant help. "Jesus," said in reverence, is a powerful prayer in itself. It stops the enemy in his tracks and sends him fleeing. A person in his sick bed repeating the name, "Jesus," brings My Son's immediate presence, with healing in His wings. A dying man uttering the name is blessed with My Son's anointing presence. Habitual use of this majestic name adds graces upon graces. Its power is beyond human comprehension. It can be used as a tool to carve your own destiny. Used the wrong way, as a curse, it brings damnation to the soul. I want My people to teach others the values of using the name above all names, "Jesus."

February 17

Muster up courage to live in My will and exercise holiness. A satisfaction with self will ensue which breeds contentment. This type of person becomes My best servant. My people will take note and receive such a person with great confidence. This quality enables My servants to receive a great following. I can thus use this person in many ways. Working for Me is a high honor bestowed from Heaven. Earth people may try to dissuade you from being My servant. Recognition may not be your lot. But the glory awaiting you in your eternal home will be worth it all. I have a crown of precious stones waiting for each one who unselfishly serves Me. Inwardly you have a knowing of who you are. Some of you have had to take detours but they have been for your own good. Keep pressing on in your limited state toward your crown.

February 18

Rekindle the fire of love in you. Keep it burning at all times. My people need the warmth from this love. They cry out for it. My words when ingested can melt the hardened hearts. Tears often accompany the thawing of these frozen hearts. It is then I can take over and refurbish what the world destroyed. Pray for a warm heart to keep the enemy from turning it hard. Prayer accomplishes much in your heart which spreads to others. The heart is the most important organ in man. Functioning properly in My spirit, it beats with the heavenly sounds and pleases My ears. The heart controls man's actions. Man's works reveal the true nature of the heart. Perfect works unite your heart and mine to beat as one.

February 19

In the midst of your storms I am with you. Believe this and I will give you My wings to rise above them. Just as Peter walked on the water so you too can do likewise. He did not begin to sink until He took his eyes off of Me, his source. Keep your eyes and thoughts on Me and you too will not sink. You will sail through your problems and come out stronger in character. All of your trials, acted upon in this way, brings you closer to your eternal destiny. Think of your life as a ladder to climb with each rung as a trial. Never look back but keep climbing, knowing I will be at the top rung to welcome you into your eternal home.

February 20

Be of good cheer. You have won the battle. Eternity will be yours. Bring others with you. When My apostles reach this plateau, they can add merit upon merit, for My storehouse is full. Work quietly among My people with a listening ear. I will open new doors for you. Dream on about your future home in the sky. It will keep your spirits high. Put on your armor each day to seal your protection. The invisible shield that separates us will become more transparent. Things that seemed impossible will become more possible to you.

Your belief has brought you this far. More will be unfolded to you in due season. Be not anxious, but relax in the life I have chosen for you. It is one of fulfillment, as you will see. I take delight in watching My righteous handle the gifts I have bestowed upon them, especially the excitement that bubbles up from the heart. In turn, they want to give of their gifts. I know ahead who will do this and that is why I call My people My chosen ones.

February 21

There are so many people in your world that are hurting. Tell them to come to Me just as they are and not to wait. Many think they will come to Me later so they do not want to give up their sinful habits. They are not at peace and are extremely unhappy and lonely. You may be just the one to turn their life around. If they would call out to Me with a repenting heart, I would help them confiscate their sinful past. The peace that I can give them can anchor their lives and stabilize their emotions. This is the new life that brings about remarkable changes and becomes recognizable by their acquaintances. Do not hesitate to speak of My loving forgiveness. Time is of the essence. Use it wisely by saving as many souls as you can. Releasing your time spreading the word will cause Me to open the windows from Heaven and pour out My blessings upon you.

February 22

All good gifts come from above. Ponder on this, recalling your blessings. The food that you take for granted, the clothing, the housing and the transportation are all gifts. There are whole deprived countries that lack all these so-called essentials. My expectancy for these gifts is a thankful heart. Many of My people have an abundance of earth's gifts. These must be shared if they want to stay in My will. Pray for a softened heart that it will not succumb to earth's luxuries. Give and I will see that you keep receiving. This is My law of reciprocity. To sit back and enjoy all the riches is not what you were created to do. You were made to serve Me during your earthly life. My wishes for you are all in My word. Happy are those who find them and put them into practice. My sustaining grace will keep them close to Me during their lives' journeys.

February 23

As you journey with Me, I will increase and you will decrease. Your focus will become more and more on Me. Self will be put into the background. Pleasing Me will become your number one aim in life. You will become sensitive to all My desires. My ways will become your ways. Some may frown on your actions but others will try to imitate them. Follow your own convictions. Your life is being directed by Me. Listen not to the evil one that tries to pull you from My gravity. Deny self at times to build stamina for My greater works. Do not push ahead of Me with over-ambition to serve. My wish for you may be to take spells of rest in My love. The body breaks down when overtaxed. I often had to go to a secluded spot to rest and pray. Resting is not a waste of time but rather keeps the body from wasting away. Walking and talking with Me brings a slower restful peace and pace into your life. Take these daily moments of practice. The more you practice My presence, the more your life in the spirit will grow, taking you to greater heights.

February 24

Your faith will make you whole. It comes by hearing My word. Rationalize all you hear and read My word, meditating on it day and night. It brings healing to the mind and soul. My incumbents learn to cherish My word and hold onto it as an anchor and stabilize themselves in all their thoughts and actions. Claiming it overcomes evil. Learn to discern good and evil. Those who hunger for My word become satisfied, for I am the bread of life. Keep your acquired knowledge on your lips and share with others. The world is hungry for the truth that will set them free. By seeking My Kingdom you will have everything else added unto you. Aspire, My loved one.

February 25

Reiterate your values and sustain your concepts. Your resurrected Lord is among you, healing and delivering. Be not frightened or alarmed at the unseemly events taking place. They are all signs of the times warning you of My imminent return. Some events may astound you but attention has to be aroused. Interpose good to thwart evil. The erosion of lives is multiplying rapidly. My people can reshape the world if they band together in one accord. Systematize organized laws to correspond to My word. This can be accomplished with prayer and self denial and the dropping of all barriers. My will shall then be accomplished more speedily and contamination can make an about-face.

February 26

Backsliding is an abomination to your Christian growth. It reveals your true character. Reorientate your life and make it conform to My word. Stamp out your inconsistencies. Renew your Baptismal vows. 'Stick-to-itiveness' is the answer. The so-called "wishey-washey" people will never make it to My kingdom. It takes a strong will and determination to keep going in spite of the odds. To those that walk My straight and narrow path I will show My love and compassion. They will become ever more sensitive to My presence. They will become true servants that I can use to mold and further the work of My Kingdom. My light will shine on all the paths they tread. Nothing will become too hard for them. This is My assurance for doing My will. The slogan to follow is "onward and upward."

February 27

Reeducate the mind to conform with the spirit. True metamorphosis will emerge. The mind fights with the spirit as it has a tendency to figure out things in a scientific manner. With faith you believe what you hear even though you cannot see it. My apostle, Thomas, had to see the nail scars in My hands before He would believe that I had risen from the dead. Blessed are My followers who believe My word and accept it as the truth. I can make the impossible come to pass if you believe without doubting. I know what is in the heart. I heal today just as I did 2,000 years ago, often working through My anointed people as instruments. Any doubt of this fact will not bring about a healing. Believe with all your heart and you shall receive for I make things come to pass. Increasing your prayer life stirs up the fire of faith. Then reading My word begins to make sense to you and you see through the eyes of faith. The zeal to grow spiritually is a gift from Me. You can pray for this gift and I will not withhold it. Your life will begin taking on a new dimension, one you would not have dreamed possible.

February 28

Eradicate the blemishes in your life and do not try covering them up. I, your God, see all and know all. You are stigmatized, so do not think that you are getting away with anything. Put your whole life out in the open before Me, faults and all. Give them all over to Me. I can then help you with them, one by one. If you are not ready to give them all up, then I will not come to your assistance. Unless I am invited in, I stay away. Blessed are those who call upon Me. Often I send My angels to rescue them. My gravitation is drawing them up to a higher plateau of holiness. They become children of My Heavenly family although still on earth. Their benefits are unlimited. No super insurance policy could ever equal My beneficial claims for them. I love all people so much and am waiting patiently to rehabilitate them. The only requirement is that they ask with a penitent heart.

MARCH

March 1

Let your face radiate with My love. I have eradicated unpleasant experiences from your memory. Do not look back with regrets, but only forward with eager anticipation of only good things happening. Revitalize yourself with quiet moments with Me. Work harmoniously with all the people I place in your path. Synchronize your thoughts to agree with My word. Analyze all your meditations. Certain figments of your thoughts can be uprooted and new seeds planted. The new growth can sprout an improved character, one made more in My image and likeness. Let love saturate your whole being, for love of Me and love of your neighbor are My two greatest commandments. Resolve to spread this love in every way possible, knowing My heavenly approval will bring you rich rewards and blessings.

March 2

Vanquish your pride and begin relinquishing your worldly ties. Work at becoming humble. Seek not your own but seek the welfare of others. Substantiate your actions in accordance with My word. Make atonement for past mistakes by giving unselfishly to My people. Be tender and affectionate and it will be recognizable from above. Working on faults always brings about My approval. Let love radiate through you to others. The configuration of your character will bring the attention of your family and friends. Strive earnestly to please Me and My grace and power, when requested, will be given to you freely. My power can lift you out of your limited state. I reveal Myself to My righteous in unusual ways. Look forward to this with expectancy and you will not be disappointed. Never stop growing, My dear, but keep pushing on toward your high calling.

March 3

Commensurate with your ability, announce the good news of My imminent return. Take a personal interest in each person you contact. Good rapport generates good relationships and trusting friends. Do not hold back your witnessing for My people are hungry. Tell them to untie the knots that hold them from a spiritual growth with Me. I long for each one's companionship. I can gratify their deepest desires. My peace will penetrate their souls if only they ask for it. They begin to understand that trials are only stepping stones to eternity. With this knowledge they can bear the weight and stay on top of them instead of being pulled down. All of My people are in the driver's seats of their own destinies. Shifting to high gear will cause them to soar to heights unknown. Pray for motivation and I will supply the props when needed. Your life can become full of adventure when we walk through the valleys and mountains together.

March 4

Regulate your life in conformance with My standards. This takes constant awareness on your part. Living in accordance with My word brings about a disciplined life. There are many stumbling blocks in life but I can lift you up and over them, just keep your eyes on Me. Gratification to self comes only by doing My will. Worldly desires can soon lose their spark and an emptiness prevails. Try Me and you will find I am the answer. This takes diligent seeking on your part, with a determination to do things My way, since you know deep down in your heart it is the best way. People on the worldly merry-go-round must stop going in circles and take inventory of their life. If they ask for My help, we can rebuild that life together. I will then make the cross-over to eternal life one of eager anticipation.

March 5

I love you. You are My worker abiding in Me. Your years will melt off because of your devotion and willingness to serve Me. Keep praying for all My people. You have no idea of the tremendous value this accomplishes, both for yourself and for the people. My blessing and protection is upon you day and night. All your sacrifices are acknowledged. Your writings are being inspired from above and you will aspire through them. Have a happy day! I will travel with you always. Your life will continue to have meaning because you are devoting it to My cause. The Heavens are being unveiled to you. When dark days seem to come upon you, read this and it will slide you over the hump. Life continues to have its storms, but you can stay above them with practice.

March 6

My word motivates people to be perfect as I am perfect. When My people desire this perfection, I infuse into them a new heart. I cleanse them with My eternal living water and make them into a new creature. At this stage there is no turning back on their part. I then work with them as a potter works with clay, molding until I set the desired image. This takes time but I never give up. Each one is unique and I handle everyone in a different manner. When they begin reflecting My image, I use them as My servants and work through them to accomplish My purposes, increasing their gifts and talents and supplying them with ever increasing power. They will possess dignity in their world as well as reign with Me in the eternal world.

March 7

Generate happiness and you will be in demand. A laughing heart is a peaceful heart and one that does not get unruffled by circumstances. My presence abides with this type of heart. A calm assurance will accompany such a one. Burdens and cares should be given over to Me. With this trusting heart one can keep in this merry mood. Being cheerful to others becomes infectious and imparts joy. This joy is My gift to My trusting souls. So let laughter ring out and draw souls to Me. Too many people keep themselves in a sad state. They let the cares of life weigh them down. My righteous people are happy people and full of My glory.

March 8

Your transgressions will no longer be in My remembrance when you confess your sins with heartfelt repentance. The atonement has already been made by Me. Every sinner can start life anew with Me. The heavy load of sin does not have to be carried. If only people would believe this. I forgive sinners today just as I did when I walked the earth. I mingled among the sinners just waiting for them to ask My forgiveness. Some think that after so many years of sin they are doomed. I forgave the thief on the cross. All He did was ask. I told the prostitute that her sins were forgiven and to go and sin no more. How I long to do this for every sinner. There is rejoicing in Heaven every time a sinner repents.

March 9

My word has been handed down for centuries. Read it with diligence and I shall reveal myself to you. I block out the understanding of the rebellious, but with the simple, humble and obedient that are seeking, I open their eyes and ears to My truths. Blessed are they who hear My word and act upon it. Reading the Number 1 Book can become an adventure for you. Even your mind can be renewed and strengthened for your spirit enlightens your mind. Believe and you will receive beyond your expectations. The translations down through the years have all been inspired to conform to your present-day realities. Life's tensions can be lifted when you get lost in My word for My word has healing power. By reading it My people will not go hungry for I will fill them to overflowing and rekindle their love. My heavenly unction will soothe the mind and body while My words enrich the soul. Your Bible should be your trademark.

March 10

My grace is with you always. I give it out freely to My righteous. It goes with you in battle and you can come out a victor. It keeps you close to Me and makes you feel secure. Inheriting this grace is belonging to My Union, dues free. You are entitled to My numerous advantages and compensations. Your membership is valuable and unites us as one. If you stumble and fall, as so many people do, I will pick you up. My grace is your security blanket, covering you with protection and saving you for that final day when we can be reunited in My heavenly abode.

March 11

The simplicity of your spirit will carry you down life's paths. Rejuvenate your mind and let the spirit take control. With great fortitude and provisions from above, you can conquer every problem in life as it occurs. Your stamina will surprise you when your spirit has the reigns. Continual prayer will keep you in the spirit. Letting the world take precedence shifts you in a worldly gear and control of the spirit is lost. Values become obscure. Culminate quiet times with Me to cultivate the spirit. Your health will abound as the spirit grows. Your earth will grow dim as My universe opens up to you. Thus, vacating the old man and putting on the new. My streams of life carry the flow in the right direction. Blessed are you who are experiencing this flow and understand what I am conveying.

March 12

Do not give in to despondency. Relinquish all your cares and problems to Me and My solutions will astound you. Surge forward with the determination that My way will be the most welcome. Often your way would lead to a catastrophic ending. Leaving everything in My hands frees you and you are not inhibited from your capabilities. Your trust extends My power. I can reconstruct your life. Age will not be a barrier. The more you render to Me, the more I can multiply back to you. Cease to recount past mistakes. Muster up courage to grow spiritually and the pieces in your puzzle of life will fall into the right places. Your contentment from this will be heart-warming. You will have a knowing, with no doubts attached, that your eternity will be spent with Me.

March 13

I know all your thoughts even before they come into being. Not one single iota can be hidden from Me. I long to be in My people's thoughts but unfortunately worldly matters occupy the mind for the majority of the time. Lives could be changed drastically if I occupied that worldly place. Most people do not build up their faith enough to experience this fact. Treasure your time with Me and sacrifice more and more of it for Me for I can make it count toward your eternity. Time with Me is never wasted. But, oh, how much time is lost foolishly. Those who use time wisely have great insight from above. Ponder this and subject yourself to change. Let your time be of a stimulating nature, becoming twofold, pleasing both self and Me.

March 14

Let your outlook be in the futuristic range. Present situations are not lasting. The abhorring conditions some of you are enduring are fleeting. Steadfast endurance will reap for you a great harvest. If My loved ones could see their prize, their happiness would not be containable. I must ask you to continue in faith, knowing My harvest will soon take place. My compassion is upon you so keep on holding on. I fulfill My promises to My righteous. I am more overjoyed to give out your rewards than you can possibly realize. What a happy Jubilee Day we shall have when we see each other face to face.

March 15

My faithful incumbents do not deviate from My laws but abide by them, following them explicitly. It is this type I use to work through as My instruments. Their commitment to Me is their registration for supernatural works which require My power. They become My empty vessels which I delight to fill. In their super accomplishments they give Me all honor and glory. Their example can stir the less fortunate to desire holiness. What seems to be unreality can take shape into reality when My spiritual people are anointed from above. This is why believers receive. They do not limit My powers. Great and mighty things become possible for I manifest Myself through them. Do not underestimate the potential of My power when our spirits unite.

March 16

Revolutionize My people where you can. Do not hesitate to revolt when you hear something that is not according to My principles. I want My people to speak up for My cause. I implant boldness in My present-day apostles. There are so many hurting people who need to be reached. I infuse the characteristics needed in those that will spread My gospel. There are the lukewarm people who live just for the flesh, strictly for self gratification. This type will have no place in My kingdom. This type could be changed if My people would heed to My call and step out in faith. They will be furnished the gifts needed to carry on My work. Let your spirit become attuned to My voice. Sometimes I speak to you through others. Be alert and recognize My call. I need an army to go to battle to help save souls in these last days.

March 17

Order your ideas to conform to My word. Hold fast to your belief in Me for I am the way, the truth and the life. Do not be swayed by conversation, but stick to your convictions. I have given you grace to believe along with opening up your spiritual eyes and ears. Many of your counterparts have not had the special opportunity that I have bestowed upon you. Your prayerful life has opened the door to My special blessings. Keep believing and you will keep receiving. My flame of fire enkindled in you will ignite when needed. You have My assurance of My constant presence. Fear no longer should play a part in you. Your ever impending theme song should be "Trust in the Lord."

March 18

Cast all your cares upon Me. If you give not your problems over to Me and trust Me with them, I will do nothing about them. By waiting on Me and allowing Me to handle them, you can be sure that I have your best interest at heart. Eternal values are put into play. Be cognizant that all things are working together for your own good. Complacent people do nothing to bring about action from above. I come to the rescue of those who storm the heavens with their prayers. Action on your part is a prime requisite. Doing your part according to My principles brings about quicker solutions. Then question not the outcome, knowing I am in it and your Father knows best. I sleep not but watch over My children, those that have placed complete trust in Me. Be mobile to My answers for your prayers. They may be contrary to your desires. Comply daily with My laws and My peace will be upon you.

March 19

I look for thanks and praise from My people. The benefits derived are insurmountable for you, both in this world and the next. Praise Me no matter what the circumstances. Our relationship becomes enriched as I listen to your praises. It brings about a joyful heart which in turn becomes a thankful heart. You do not need the riches of your world to obtain such a heart. Make thanks and praise a daily ritual and I'll pour out My blessings upon you. This will bring about My wonderful peace, the peace that surpasses human understanding. Many daily routines could be eliminated to make room for the things that count in My number system. Set new goals, those that can lead you to your eternal reward. You will discover then that you have not lived in vain. Recaptivate the reason for your creation, that of knowing, loving and serving Me so you can be happy with Me in Heaven.

March 20

The world has transient values. Discard these values and transcend your thoughts to conform with My word. Diligent seeking will produce your answers. Give preeminence to My teachings. Make restitution to all possible that you have offended. Do no procrastinate in this respect. New love relationships will transpire. It is mandate that you assemble with people to witness and share for I will make the seeds fertile that you plant. Remain loving so no agitation can occur. Rotate your priorities and life can remain interesting. Coordinate with superiors. Often I speak through them. Spend much time soaking in prayer. Expedient answers will follow. Hibernate at times to keep motivated in My word. Then keep others aroused by spreading it. I need workers, for My vineyard is ripe. Immerse yourself in My service. The compensation exceeds any earthly pay.

March 21

Transfix your gaze on the cross often. It has therapeutic effects. Confine yourself to moments of dwelling on My passion. You will begin to comprehend the love I have for My people. I paid the price for their salvation. Through the cross, I made it possible for My righteous to have the indwelling of My spirit. This spirit guides you along the paths of life and reveals truths to you. I paid the price for everyone's sins. All people have to do is ask forgiveness. Now you know the depth for My suffering. So look to the cross often with eyes of veneration. Leave your problems at the foot of My cross. Knowing that you face eternal life lifts the burdens of those problems. Leaving them with Me shows your trust. Count My many blessings and I'll carry you through on My wings.

March 22

I am drawing My righteous closer to Me day by day. You are beginning to understand the meaning of life and the vastness of My universe. The temptations of your world no longer affect you. Your only desire is to please Me. I delight in My righteous that reach this stage. I place them on My pedestal which I lift higher and higher. The ecstasy you are experiencing is My gift to you. In spite of the thorns that come into your life, they will no longer phase you. You are also enjoying the beauty around, which at one time you took for granted and never fully appreciated. Your time is now used wisely. Greater tasks will you be given because you have proven your dependability. My angels have been given charge over you so you have assured protection from above. With your new created heart, you have the power to draw others to My Kingdom.

March 23

I light the paths which My people trod. They no longer walk in darkness. Their spiritual eyes have been open to see and comprehend My truths. They are given insight into the depth of My word. Their perception becomes keen. Those who wish to obtain this should seek diligently to mend their ways. I will not withhold things from sinners who make an earnest effort to change. As I allow My light to seep into my people, My word becomes logical to them. They wonder why they did not see My open truths before. Through their open mind and constant seeking, I open up a new world to them. Once on this road, they do not want to turn back. Their growth has begun. As My light becomes brighter in you, it lights the paths of those around you. My people shine as they absorb more and more light. After darkness has been eliminated, they enter into a joyful eternal life which can be experienced yet in your world. When I call them home, they just step over the threshold and death has no sting. My people look forward to dying for they know that their acquired knowledge of the hereafter will become reality. They have learned to look forward with eager anticipation for the great ramification of their heritage.

March 24

Do not stagnate. Keep your mind aroused with My truths. Culminate the habit of collecting knowledge. This will keep the mind active. Do research studies on foods so your body can be nourished along with your mind. Then remember that your thirsting soul can only be satisfied by Me. I tremble for the people that pay no attention to Me. Do not wait for old age to creep in before returning back to Me for long-time habits have driven you further and further away. The evil one will tell you it is too late and, since you have listened to his deceiving for many years, you tend to believe his deceptions. Reestablish sound doctrine before it is too late. Call while I am within hearing distance. My righteous have My presence at all times. They are blessed beyond measure. I will lead you into stable ways and contentment will be your lot. You can get delivered from all vexations. Retaliate to safer, higher grounds while you can. Then tune in on My wavelength. The high frequency has a lifting effect.

March 25

Refrain from judging others. Earthly people do not know all the circumstances involved. Instead of judging, pray for the persons that antagonize you. This immediately starts supernatural powers working for the welfare of the person as well as benefiting your own character. Treasure your prayer time for it quiets the mind and soul. I can mellow the fight-back attitude that judgment so often brings. Quick tempered people should pray and ask for My deliverance before ill health takes over. Temper can stir up entire bodily functions. With this knowledge, help can come to your rescue from above if only you ask. My righteous people have been set free from this bad habit through prayer and patient endurance. Renounce bad habits, working on them one by one, and you can become an overcomer in all fields. This is the road to holiness that increases blessing from above.

March 26

Your earthly decisions can be turned in the right direction through prayer. Often your own desires would not lead to the best I had in mind for you. Praying about everything opens up new avenues for you. Impossibilities become possibilities. I know more what My people are suited for than they know. Wanting your own way could even lead to sin. Anchoring oneself in My word brings about positive answers. It guides your spirit in ways in which you can live more abundantly. It will transform your thoughts to coincide with My thoughts. Your new mind can be trained to be in harmony with My will. I delight in watching My people change spiritually. They are renovated into new creatures, thus improving their environment and bringing joy and self-satisfaction upon themselves.

March 27

I am the remedy for all your problems. Be Christ oriented by placing Me in the center of your life. Live one day at a time following My commandments. The ease of conscience stimulates a song in your heart. You are no longer weighed down with earth's problems. Knowing Me keeps you in the Spirit and Spirit is life. Your only hope is in Me, so rest in Me, trusting all is well because you have made Me the Lord of your life. People's lives become complex because they leave Me out and try to solve their own problems. They become disenchanted with the world and disappointed in people. I am your divine inspiration, all in all. Happy the man who makes this discovery early in life. He is vindicated from confusion, thus leaving his burdens light. He refuses to worry and makes Me his goal in life. He knows I will not fail him.

March 28

I know all your thoughts, actions and good deeds. None is hidden from Me. Prostrate yourself before Me in adoration. Times like these please Me greatly. I honor all your praises and highly exalt you. Your fount of life will never run dry. It will spill over into other channels, cleansing My people from all unrighteousness. Pray, for the time is evil. The wicked are becoming more wicked, carrying the weak with them. My righteous are given the power to pick up the weak if only they would adhere to My promptings. I died to save souls. Be willing to go through discomfort for your fellowmen. My missionaries always need help. Reach out to all My people in faith, doing all you can, and I will meet your good endeavors, carrying them to completion. No one can wipe your good deeds from My slate.

March 29

Disengage yourself from earthly pleasures. They are needless when My spirit abounds in you. Crossing over My line of demarcation transcends ascetic moments of bliss which surpass fleeting earthly pleasures. Dote on the glorious future I have in store for you. That is a dream no one can steal from you. My Heavenly choirs have a majestic sound that no one on the earth is capable of producing. Even the most beautiful painting on earth could never portray the magnificence of Heaven. This will be all yours to enjoy for ever and ever. Can you see why I want you to draw people to Me? The love I have implanted in you should spur you on to stir the hearts of the faithful to seek their eternal reward, no matter what the cost on earth will be to attain it. Even the perfect health state should be incentive enough to go all out for the prize.

March 30

Theorize My word as good common sense mingled with wisdom. Problems are minimized when My word is applied. Your knowledge is coagulated, with all your bodily functions determining your health. Consternation does not overpower those who are well grounded in My word. Your focal point should be Me. Anyone or anything else is folly. With the degree put forth is the degree with which you will harvest. No efforts made in My name are ever a loss. I prod My people along, sending them encouragement. They have an option, though, and at times slip away. But I am the Good Shepherd and patiently gather up My lost sheep to the fold when they repent. Frequent prayer and meditation brings one closer and closer to His eternal destiny.

March 31

Fondle your moments with Me. They should captivate your whole being. I can redirect your life when you are going off course. Cease trying to do things yourself. Contemplate all your motives with Me to keep them pure. Call on Me any time of day or night and you will have Me at the helm steering you on the right course. Let Me fulfill your desires. Just wait on Me. I can rebuild your hopes and dreams. Your environment can be changed when you are subject to change. Then, fear not these changes. When you are operating in My will, they are sanctioned by Me. Go forth with boldness and you will overpower the enemy. Great and mighty things will you do, for My power has no limits when operating through you to accomplish My purposes.

APRIL

April 1

Negotiate with Christian people. Financial situations can be handled in a just manner because they have learned My commandment of love. Business deals can be collated to correspond to My principles. Laws have been enacted down through the ages to reestablish just policies but unfortunately some of the so-called lawyers and politicians find shady ways of their own and injustice is put into play. Taxes are another detriment to fair play. My rule still holds from My word, "Render to Caesar the things that are Caesar's and to God the things that are God's." No matter how subtle the method, everything you do is on record above. Always generate fair policies. Then your conscience can keep you in perfect peace, and rest can be your lot.

April 2

Timidity can be overcome with determination, hard work and prayer. Any project backed by prayer brings My intervention. Some resolutions may not be understandable to the naked mind but do not dwell on the matter. Keep the mind active in prayer and constructive thinking will always be put to play. Thus, worry is eliminated from the scene. Mastering any problem becomes an art when I am brought into the picture. Always be submissive to My will. My good Book contains all your answers. Seek devoutly for knowledge and help from above will be attainable. Anyone well versed in My word is My disciple. Go therefore and teach with the gifts I have bestowed upon you. Just remember, My rewards are unlimited.

April 3

The mind must be kept active or it can become incapacitated. When My people are no longer in the working class they have a tendency to relax their mind. It can get out of order just as the body when not used. Keep movements going at all times in spite of sickness that may creep in upon you. Many illnesses can be overcome with the determination not to give in to the symptoms. Even My medical doctors are not infallible on their diagnoses. Pray and keep fighting attacks of any disease. With My help and your faith in Me, sickness can be lifted. Never give up. Keep on trusting. Do everything for your body and mind that is humanly possible and My divine will can take over from there.

April 4

Let your life-style reveal My love. By being loving yourself you reflect My image to others. Maintain a cheerful disposition no matter your feelings. This will automatically lift your spirit and the spirit of those around you. Be a true friend to all I send you. You may be entertaining angels. Give generously of your time and money and it will be increased back to you. There may be times you feel dry of spiritual nourishment but I am still with you, watching your every move. Feed upon spiritual food and I will see that you always have plenty. Your commitment to Me will bring about unusual results. My people have a variety of stories when they witness for Me for I reveal Myself in unusual ways and circumstances. Compare your stories and never stop listening, growing and expecting.

April 5

The artifice of Christianity is knowing the truth that sets you free. This knowledge, ingrained in your mind, keeps you ever refreshed. It can only be obtained by an ever open mind to the word of God. People can become brave to the point of dying for their faith. The early Christians were true examples of this fact. The consistency of prayer brings you closer to being a true Christian. Keeping the mind active in My word develops its true potential. My followers develop the undaunted urge to grow in My likeness. They are given an ever increasing courage to speak out in My name. Converts are drawn by the magnetic influence I implant in My believers. Seek to ever widen your knowledge in My word and devote your time to spreading it. Your beckoning will have My immediate attention. This assurance is great gain on your part.

April 6

Strive to measure up to the standards in the big, as well as the small things in life. The felicity of your cooperation in this shall ever blossom your character. Measuring up to My standards is My followers' aim in life. I will plant the seeds to bring about their desired results. A gradual transformation will take place. "Patience" becomes a must in the development. Their growth in grace and virtue is a continual ongoing process bestowed from above. Spiritual efforts are always rewarded. I calmed the tempestuous seas and My people can have this calming effect on people's lives, often causing a complete turnaround. Keep in mind that it is your great faith in Me that brings about these changes and your undying love that activates them.

April 7

My love has no bounds. What I do for others I can do for you. Ask in anticipation and you will receive, if backed by faith. Resignation to My will, coupled with an earnest effort to stay free from sin, brings many favors from above. The radiation of My love united with yours can bring untold gifts. Often you will find you are able to do things that you never dreamed possible. Consider this a gift from your creator. You are then to use these gifts for the betterment of others and not for self-gain. If you live your life to please Me, I will make your life pleasurable. My love has no limits. Often experiencing this love changes your whole outlook on life. My people acquire real happiness when they use their gifts for spiritual advancement for themselves and for others. This happiness can fulfill the innermost longings of your heart.

April 8

Pray for My peace. It will keep you in a tranquil state no matter the circumstances around you. Worry and anxiety vanish for you have the realization that nothing in your world is lasting. Sickness can be combatted for you know I have the power to alleviate symptoms. By not concentrating on the disease and trusting in Me completely, believing that all things are possible and that I am a God of miracles, My peace can remain with you in diverse conditions. People with My peace have a knowing that this life is fleeting and they are only looking forward to the beautiful life ahead. They will do the best they can and count on My word to fill their lack. If you have attained this peace, count yourself among My elect.

April 9

My people must learn proper food assimilation. They should eat to live, not live to eat. A normal weight can be maintained if one does not let gluttony take precedence. If one is too thin, it is one's duty to get proper nourishment. Often health breaks down from lack of food knowledge. Many people form sinful eating habits. Pray for My guidance and do not give in to self-gratification. Fasting can be good for both body and soul. You are your own keeper of these two most vital forms of life. Self-control is the key to My kingdom and it can only come with practice. Body abuse is a sin. My people must diligently seek My forgiveness and take measures to correct their food and drink intake.

April 10

When My people are gathered together to sing praises to Me, I am walking among them, pouring out My blessing upon them. This strengthens them to cope with their problems. The inner man receives the will to go on and continue running the race in life, adding rich rewards to his eternal account. My people do not break down under pressure for they can draw from that inner strength I place in them as a gift. Praising is a need in your everyday life and singing praises gives you double blessings. Cease not to build the inner man because one day it will rise again, just as I did in My resurrection.

April 11

Maintain an even disposition to keep yourself in a healthy state. Cooperate with everyone in all that is good and just. Take an interest in people around you and become a good listener. I send certain people into your life for your spiritual development. Expect to receive spiritual gifts when you ask and I will fulfill the desires of your heart. Prolong our visits together and keep them free of distraction. I long for your companionship. Your thinking will begin acquiring My inspiration. Your outlook on life will attain a broader scope, one in line with My word. Your charisma will improve as our relationship develops. The more we commune, the more My influential spirit will unite with yours. You will be kept in tune with eternal matters. Transmit your ever increasing knowledge to My starving people.

April 12

Learn to recognize spiritual needs in others and pray to Me for guidance to meet those needs. Leading someone to Me can be profitable to both of us. Praying about the matter supplies you with My grace to aid the person in the right manner. I, too, can work in that person to bring about a receptive mind and heart. Working alone cannot bring about your desired results. Don't give up if that person becomes indignant but keep praying for him. In My due season the conversion will take place. I listen and answer My children's pleas in ways that are more suitable for their soul. Do not despair. It will occur even if it be their last hour. I am a rewarder of your patience and endurance.

April 13

The unification of our fellowship is of a divine origin. Your creation was miraculous and accompanied by My breath of life. I treasure each individual but give them a free will. Unfortunately most go their own way with no thought of Me or tomorrow. They must be awakened before it is too late. Each person's stewardship is needed to wage a war against the evil which is becoming more rampant in these last days. My righteous have jobs to fulfill and I will supply the power. Those who trust Me for this power will receive it. Everyone's hard work and sacrifice will be rewarded. They will receive joy while on the earth and high honors in My Kingdom. Pray for My gifts so that you can be entitled to these honors. Work is involved on your part but the glory in eternity is beyond all comprehension.

April 14

The tensions of everyday living drag people down but those who have My spirit can function well. Promulgate good praying habits and stick to them. Praying for others to be healed brings your own healing. Treat others with tenderness and they will reciprocate. Systems enacted on My behalf have My blessings upon them. Venturing out into your world, trusting Me, brings about exciting living, minus the worry. Always pray for My grace for with it your life can become a conquering adventure. Expect My power and I will supply it.

The wonderment of the results brings about total amazement to My followers plus a self-satisfaction that your world alone could never give.

April 15

I am pouring out My gifts on many in these last days. I want them to be used to wake up those that are asleep. Many are not aware of what is taking place. I am working among all the faithful that are gathered together in My name. Use your spiritual gifts and I will develop them to further My Kingdom. Announce the good news of My imminent return. Let your voice reverberate so the deaf ears will be opened. Live your life in a holy manner, ever joyful and thankful for the blessings you have already received. Watchful eyes are upon My servants so let your example exemplify My gifts. Your words are My words. Use them for gathering souls, continually asking for My blessings upon them. Step out in holy boldness.

April 16

My followers remain peaceful no matter their state of life. They have learned to trust in Me. They weather the storms of life with courage and realize I am with them through it all. Their goals are not set high on earthly matters but are set high on things above. Those who go through pain and hardship with patience are My dearest friends. They have experienced a taste of My sufferings and our unity becomes one. This is a high honor for My earthly loved ones. Those who offer up their suffering for My people will share in My resurrection power. Measuring up to My standards is a hard road to travel but one of immeasurable compensations. So struggle on, My loved ones, with fortitude and determination and you will reach the high standards set before you.

April 17

Be a person that welcomes change. It can expand the personality. Changes in praying can increase your prayer life. Growth brings about changes and we must be willing to bend. If one becomes set in one's ways, that person's growth becomes impaired. Learn to discipline your prayer life, finding time to walk and talk with Me each day and give Me thanks and praise for all your blessings. Become a master of your body and soul rising above the self-life. The shaded areas of your life can disappear with will power. Calling on Me for help in all your endeavors will bring about our desired results. Subject yourself to My leadings for they will be varied. Your openness is above reproach. I am using you as My vessel and will fill it to overflowing.

April 18

Keep temper under control at all times. Dispel from your mind any ill thoughts about your neighbor. Bitterness held inwardly can bring about illness. Rid your mind of such thoughts and ask My forgiveness. All judgment should be left for Me. "Love everyone" is My commandment. Pray for anyone who irritates you and I can lift their irksome habits. Resignation to My will removes worry and discontentment. Reach out to others with the surety that I am in it. Time will not play heavily on your hands but will pass speedily while you are doing good deeds. Pleasing others in the long run pleases yourself also. Discussing your heartaches with Me can lift them faster than discussing them with your neighbor. Search your heart and try Me. I am your answer.

April 19

Laugh at your past life, with all its hardships and mistakes, and you will not look back with regrets, but only onward with eager anticipation, knowing I walk with you. I'll take you to new adventures with heights unlimited. You will discover that the touch of your Master's hand makes the difference. You will find that your kindness will increase, adding joy and satisfaction to your everyday life. Recreate new interests, especially digging into My word for answers. "He who seeks will find" brings about a fascination. Ask favors of Me and, if they be for your good, they will be granted. Believing in Me brings about results. It is lack of belief that I shun. Rest in My protection for I never slumber.

April 20

Lasting happiness is earned, not purchased. It comes with an ease of conscience. It is the inner good feeling one receives, knowing he or she has done the best possible with the tools that I have furnished. It is the following of My commandments and the love of Me and your neighbor that brings the greatest joy. As love is given away, I keep replacing it with an increase. Love can penetrate a hardened heart. It can soothe the broken hearted and mend wounds of hurt. Never stop loving and your enlarged heart will cover a multitude of sins to where I will no longer remember them. Love conquers all. Other things fail but love fails not. So let your love radiate to all I place in your path. This is living your Christian life to the fullest.

April 21

Smoking, drinking or taking pills to experience a high is not acceptable to Me. They become habit forming, thus breaking down the health. Your body is My temple and I will not take up My abode in these people. They lack My protection. I can help if they earnestly seek deliverance from such habits. Giving it up for Me and keeping My sufferings and death on the cross ever in their mind can overcome this lustful habit. Those who never became addicted should thank Me and consider themselves blessed. They should pray for their friends and loved ones with such unruly habits. Your unending prayers can implant a strong will in the person possessing the habit and the craving can be lifted. These people should not be given up as hopeless. Time, patience and prayer conquer.

April 22

Subject yourself to quiet moments with Me. The body needs this rest. Most people set too fast a pace for themselves and body burnout develops. Stop and give up certain activities that rob you of your rest. Then remember My help is always available if you ask. Many people work themselves up over unmeaningful tasks. Take inventory and correct useless thoughts and work. Spend time on the things in life that count toward your eternity. This builds your character and you will ever be walking closer to Me. It is during our restful moments together that you receive guidance. Time with Me is well spent. Your life will be made easier and you will function with your faculties in normal gear. Your work is sanctified when offered up for Me.

April 23

Take notice of the beauty of spring, the new life of buds blossoming. I created it all for My peoples' enjoyment. Notice the intricacies of a flower. Man could never duplicate them. Listen to the chirping songs of the birds in the early morning hours and watch the beautiful sunsets in the evening. Most of My people are too involved in their work activities to enjoy My creations. These give rest and new life to the body when pondered upon. So take time to breathe in the fragrance of nature. You will then understand My greatness. Remember that you can always lean on Me for support. The lonesome feeling vanishes for those who have learned to experience My presence. The inoculations of nature can carry you through the stresses of everyday living.

April 24

Pray and keep praying. It is so important. Staying in prayer chases the darkness out of your life. Evil thoughts cannot dwell in the mind that is in prayer. While you are in the state of praying for others, I am performing a healing on you. My people have many faults but they can be overcome through prayer. Patience and endurance are two qualities I admire most. Openness to change in self-improvement brings My special help. So if you keep increasing your prayer life a remarkable change can take place. Prayer is so vital for well-being. Strive toward My word, "Be ye perfect as I am perfect."

April 25

We can bring a touch of Heaven to people on earth by our attitude. The right Christian attitude lifts the spirits of the people around us, affecting each in a special way. Grace abounds for you in any spiritual uplifting that you give to others. You alone set the theme of your attitude, whether it be positive or negative. If it is positive you will never have a lack of friends—I for one. With the right attitude the disposition remains at an even keel. A calm assurance is given to My people for they sense My presence in such a person. Evil lurks in people who have bad attitudes. Work always on maintaining the best possible attitude that you know will be pleasing to Me. You will then find favor with Me as well as with others.

April 26

As My people grow in grace they become rich in virtue. They develop great wisdom because they have been given insight from above. Their knowledge ever increases for they do not seek self-gain but reach out to others' needs and thereby learn from them. Their fortitude has been built up for they have learned how to withstand the trials and tribulations of life. Steadfastness in My word has brought them real endurance. I delight in watching My gifts of grace mold My people into My image. The newness of life enthrones them and they have no desire to step out of these boundaries. Such are My loved ones ever drawn closer to Me.

April 27

When one repents a restoration is brought to the soul. The uniting of our spirits takes place. My spirit is then your helper and your burdens in life become lighter. I counsel you in your problems so that your spirit knows the right way. I intercede for you in your dark hours. Some changes in your life will be immediate and some gradual but all will be for your good. Your key word is trust. If after repenting you choose to take up again your sinful life, I will leave you until asked back with true sorrow. Your free will determines our togetherness. Those who have taken long journeys know the richness of a close relationship with Me. My only wish is for all people to enjoy this closeness.

April 28

Continue to lift your mind and heart to Me and remember that I and My Father are One. Sin has no entrance in a mind occupied by My presence. The good things in life can be enjoyed to the utmost knowing we are in it. When life becomes a struggle, keep right on going with your head held high knowing I am carrying you through and will lift you out of the valleys. Prove Me from your past. Contentment should dominate your life. Let yours spill on My people. Your everyday contacts are important when lifting someone up is enacted. Songs of praise will ever keep you on top of your world. The animations of your actions can invigorate your soul and your body. Keep humble and lowly of heart and your heart will become like mine.

April 29

Blessed are all of you who walk in My way. Your cries are heard. I have not abandoned you. Justice will be yours. Rekindle the fire of your love in spite of your temporary hardships. Your testing grounds have been ordered for a short duration so you can be proven as gold from out of a furnace. Consider your life a contest and strive to win the first prize. Your efforts will be worth a hundredfold to you. Resume your struggle with great determination and this attitude will mount you up as an eagle soaring high in the sky. One tarries on this earth but a few moments compared to the eternal stay. Cherish our intimacies to enhance our love affair.

April 30

Your integrity will shine through all your endeavors for your prayer life has won for you immeasurable victories. Be not dismayed at future events. They are being directed by Me. Certain elements in the economy will work out for your benefit so do not hesitate to make decisions. Your coverage will be guaranteed because of your faithfulness. My people are winners. Opportunities will ever be available to you and I will follow through with the help needed. You will see that your trust has won untold favors. The unfolding of future events will astound you but you will know that I am in it all. Life need not be dull when you reach out to others in holy anticipation.

MAY

May 1

Be in constant expectancy of good things happening and they will come to pass. Goals are attainable when complete trust is placed in Me. Situations can be turned around to coincide with your thinking. I am a God of plenty waiting to give, but to appreciative hands. A restoration of the good things can be yours as you reach out to others. Reeducate My people with your newfound theories. My interventions will never cease to amaze you. Activate the fire of your love for My people and it will never burn out. Consummate all your actions in Me and they will work out for your greater glory.

May 2

Your activity in faith matters causes a chain reaction. My people observe you so let your light shine to pick up the stragglers. Example is still the best soul-winning method. We are working together but keep allowing more of Me and less of you for self must decrease. Ambitions thus shift toward eternal destination. You can determine the acceleration of people's faith around you. Never underestimate what can be accomplished when I work alongside you. Your commissioned work is to win souls and I will help set your pace. I am furnishing you the tools and depending on your wisdom for their use. Do not question the situations you are placed in but count them all as good.

May 3

Try to measure up to My expectations. They are different than those of the world. Keep always in mind the welfare of My people and act upon it. Live for My glory, not yours. I will meet each step you take to accomplish My purpose. I take out the drudgery of every task when it is offered up to Me. Your mission in life is of utmost importance so shirk not your duties. Your direction will come directly through Me with confirmation from outside sources or from My word. Often I keep My people waiting, in which case they are to stay in prayer. Patience must be practiced and is a beautiful virtue to behold. Keep yourself alert and watchful until the day of My coming.

May 4

The just shall live by faith. Faith is believing what you cannot see. The eyes can sense the reality and I can put it into being if proclaimed. This is how healings can come to pass. The unrighteous can become righteous due to the faith of a prayerful intercessor. Faith can change impossible situations. It will change the darkness into light. Rest assured that belief is your answer for successful living. This success can be obtained from belief in My word. Acting upon My word increases your faith. As it grows, the whole man develops. A new creature unfolds before My watchful eye. Faith breeds satisfaction and puts into play love, joy, peace, patience, long suffering, fortitude and endurance. This all spells happiness in spite of adversities. Most important of all, belief brings everlasting life.

May 5

Tell others that I am their way, their truth and their life. If they come to Me, I will work with them ever so gently and steer them in the right direction. One cannot be forced or pushed into being My friend. People must come to Me of their own free will with a desire to know Me better. Seeking Me they will find Me and I will open the door of their hearts. I am a God of mercy. Keep your life a living example of My love. Go out of your way for everyone even to the point of discomfort.

You will then be following in My footsteps. All your actions will be deposited in your account and you can draw on it in time of your own need. This security establishes a purpose for your own life. Rest by reading and meditating on My word each day and My strength will be given to you to carry you through from day to day. The turmoil of daily living will leave you nevertheless unruffled.

May 6

Registration to your heavenly rights is earned through your good deeds. Deep satisfaction ensues after My people perform such deeds. The connotation of their benefits earned is rewarding. Situations in life can always be altered with My interventions. Never underestimate My power and the power I can apportion to you. My generosity will overflow in My dearest friends. Keep ever close to Me and the resultant effects will never cease to astound you. I will remain your true lifelong friend, ever enriching your senses. Your keen perception will be an asset in your daily living. Dreary days will take on a sunshine effect when you acknowledge My constant presence which deepens and widens the horizons in your life. My abiding love is sustaining you day by day. Your proven worth will be recognized by others and their imitation will bring about applause from above and more blessings upon you.

May 7

I longingly await your company. Speak to Me at any time for I have a lending ear. There is so much I can do for you if you will only ask. The closer you draw to Me, the closer I will draw to you. You can be building up a protective wall around you that the enemy cannot penetrate. Our intimate meetings keep you functioning at a higher level. This lifting effect carries you from glory to glory. Your preparation to gain entrance into My world is being carried out each day. I longingly await your arrival and will welcome you with open arms.

May 8

Nothing is too hard for My faithful, trusting people. They have learned that I am in them and they are in Me. When they do their best, I come through with My best for them. When they believe this and it is deep in their spirit, they will live one day at a time in trust. Health that most people take for granted becomes a joyful, thankful reality. Reaching out to others in love opens up a whole new world. I implant in My people the desire to serve. This brings a fulfillment in their life as well as in the lives of others.

May 9

Be on call day or night, ever ready to serve. I can always use My people for intercessors. A person may come into your mind a number of times. In that case I am laying on your heart to pray for that person. Be ever alert to hear My still small voice. You must separate yourself from the world and practice My presence. Eliminating all other thoughts from your mind comes with practice. A peaceful rest is obtainable from this practice. Repeat My name with reverence over and over. The name "Jesus" is a prayer in itself. Use it often. The evil one will flee when hearing My name, taking the evil thoughts with him. Temptations are lifted because My name carries power. It stimulates your spirit and we join in a union. The results can be overwhelming.

May 10

Feature many stories that you have read and then ponder on My book, My word, which outnumbers them all. It is picking up momentum in your world's popularity. My readers' lives are affected greatly for I speak to the heart, changing the innermost desires. The greater the quantity of My word absorbed, the greater the changes. I work with each one that wills to know Me better, thus bringing about a personal relationship. Developing this is a wonderful experience and brings about untold blessings in that person's life on earth and rich rewards for all eternity. Some people put My book aside with the remark of not understanding it but, with work and effort on their part, I will bring about the comprehension necessary and an increase of faith will gradually ensue. Excuses for not reading My word rob you of many graces and blessings.

May 11

Cultivate good habits. Smiling is one that pleases Me greatly. It can lift people out of despair. Render little acts of kindness wherever possible. Consider other people's needs above your own. Learn to trust others and they will trust you. Be loving to your neighbor and it will work wonders for you.

Gentleness is another trait I admire. Also be humble and I will exalt you in due season. Comfort the sick and lonely. All these are virtuous habits that require diligence on your part. Orient yourself in the development of such practices. There will be no lack in your want for I am your rewarder.

May 12

Relax in My love. No matter the circumstances, you can always find Me in it. Enjoy each situation to the fullest. I make it all possible. Think on Me and My greatness often. Put things in My hands to be worked out by Me. You will have many surprises in your favor. Life can be made beautiful by your attitude. Rejoice that I play an ever present role to help you all the way along your journey. Prayer and praise should always be your thanksgiving.

May 13

Vocalize My messages at appropriate times. The time and circumstances will be made known to you. The building up of My people is of utmost importance. They need to be told from time to time that they are running on the right track. Venture out into the deep unknown areas and I will always pull you out, leaving My mark on those I want touched. Be willing and you will be afforded the capabilities. The issuance of My blessings far surpass the inconvenience you are put through. The creation of new hearts can be instigated through you. Never stop witnessing but push on as My servant. My will should always be present in your mind, a condition which you will learn more and more to sense.

May 14

You will walk in the light because I am in the light and I walk with you. Fear need not enter when you allow Me to be a part of your life. The evil one has a chance to go on a rampage when you leave Me out and try to operate on your own power. Continually give your life to Me and it will be one of order. Confiscate everything not of Me and then consecrate yourself wholly to Me. I am meek and gentle of heart and every one of My traits can be yours if you ask earnestly and desire them. I will hold no good thing back from you. I am the same yesterday, today and always.

May 15

Your faith will continue to supply you with My grace and protection for My gifts are poured out on My righteous. I am all merciful, so pass this on to others, especially informing the sinners. Take particular note not to judge or accuse others. Love everyone and do not make any exceptions. You will be exhorted in due season for your unfailing love. Just keep increasing it. Tenderness is a great quality to acquire. Use it on Me as well as My people. Keep yourself ever motivated toward My goals.

May 16

Be satisfied with the simple things in life. My joy is all you need. Relax knowing that this will not be taken from you. It will stimulate others so keep it flowing. Explain its origin when asked. I place curiosity in some so, in answering, My people can expound on My gifts, supplying power to excite even the unbeliever. Following through with prayer seals the explanations given and they become locked in the hearts of new or lukewarm believers. You are being watched so keep smiling and My light will shine through in your face. The winning of souls should be your prime concern. This is love working at high speed.

May 17

Judge no one and you will not be judged. Loving all people is a prime requisite for gaining entrance to My Kingdom. Enter not into conversation that degrades a person's character. Only speak to build up. Otherwise remain silent. Each one has the job of building up My Church. Retaliate from worthless positions that waste time. Make your time count toward eternal values. It is never too late to begin anew for Me. I am ever waiting to help when your decision is directed at serving Me. Affirmations will be given you so doubts will no longer have precedence in your life. Rendering yourself over to Me is only the beginning of real freedom. Bondage can no longer lord over you. Arise now and go forth with courage.

May 18

We are very close tonight. Your mind staid on Me brings this closeness. I need your time divided in listening, studying and spreading My word. It should be obvious to you now the direction of My leading. I long for My people to work with Me and have something special for each to fulfill. Each person is precious in My sight. If only they could sense this. Some completely ignore Me and this saddens Me, and to think I suffered and died for each and every person in the universe. Appreciation is what I look for but so few give thanks. The more one honors Me, the more My Father in Heaven will honor him.

May 19

Be aware that I am constantly with you in all your travels. There should be little transition in all you do. You can be anywhere and yet be at home with Me at all times. Whether high in the mountains or down in the valleys, My presence should always be felt. Weather changes should have no effect on your disposition. Learn to make the best of every situation, remembering that I am in each one. My love has no boundaries. I want to be in all your thoughts, words and actions. I can smooth out all the rough areas of your life so never hesitate to ask. I am your host and you are My host. Together we keep company. I long to be your constant companion. We shall stroll hand in hand along life's journey, crossing the bridge together on your last day.

May 20

Think on Me and the eternal rewards awaiting you and your mind will not wander. I am peace and there is only peace above so that you can stay in constant serenity. Worldly thoughts and self thoughts keep one in confusion and anxiety. The more times you practice keeping your thoughts on Me and the heavenly realm the more peace you will have accumulated. Outside pressure cannot penetrate this ecstatic state. Rest in this state often and your joy will keep overflowing. Look forward to quiet moments with Me. I long for your attention. This attention is carried over into eternity where My people never cease to adore and praise Me.

May 21

I prepare mansions in the sky for My people that eyes cannot fathom. Everything created in Heaven has beauty beyond your imagination and none of this beauty can be destroyed. It all remains spotless. My gifts are unlimited and My heavenly people want for nothing. Keep earning your way on earth by spreading My love. Drink in the beauty I have placed on your earth and you will receive a tiny particle of what is awaiting you. There is no need to fear death when righteous living has been your lot. Contemplate this and place your order on your mansion. Picture in your mind your desired furnishings and I will fulfill all your wants with a hundredfold bonus.

May 22

I created the wonders of nature for My people's enjoyment. Soak in its beauty. Let the awe of it all sink into your innermost being. My glory will reinforce your faith. Resting in this thought brings new life to the soul. Your growth in the spiritual realm enhances your life and a new meaning surfaces bringing new depth in your prayer life. Knowing I am always with you should spur you on to greater endeavors. Keep reaching out for My gifts with expectancy and your supply will keep increasing. I will not hold back from My righteous people.

May 23

I am ever creating in you a new heart. The fire of your love and mine melt into one. Tenderly we shall work with My people to build My Kingdom. No matter where I place you, content yourself knowing My purpose must be fulfilled. Converse with your friends often, telling of My love. Continue to make new friends. I will place new people in your path so welcome them. You can refresh their souls as well as they refresh your soul. Search for new fulfillment and it shall be granted you.

May 24

Keep witnessing for Me and your compensations will be overflowing. Recalling My goodness and passing it on to others reenacts My purpose on earth. My people need constant reminders or they become drifters. Hesitate not in relinquishing any information that glorifies Me. Language is one means of spreading the Gospel. My affections are lavished upon My servants who work untiringly for Me. Consecrate every act to Me and your eternal bank account will keep multiplying with interest. This is the only savings that has meaning. Unfortunately few people see through My ways. Selfishness and greed must be conquered to enable persons to earn the riches prepared for them which I earned by My sufferings and death. My servants can help in the bringing of understanding to the less fortunate. Keep reaching out to prepare for My coming.

May 25

Do not let worldly ties suffocate you. Come to Me for answers. Often I speak through others. Listen and watch for My signs. Be attentive to the spiritual intonations. Your indicated direction may not coincide with your plans but be flexible to deviate from them. Giving yourself entirely to Me will make up for many of your past mistakes and losses. I will plant your feet firmly and there will be no more stumbling. The joy I have passed on to you will alleviate some of the sorrow you might endure in your present life. Receive every gift or trial with gracious love for it is all from Me for your well being.

May 26

Those who continue to conform to My standards can weather the storms of life. Each day confirm your subjection to Me. Read My word often and not just sporadically. It takes constant effort on your part to build your faith level. Great faith removes the mountains that obstruct your view. Your faith can be contagious to others. Be in contact with people often to spread this faith. Your constant endeavors will bring about changes that you never dreamed possible. Resign yourself to this new life with enthusiasm. The benefits far exceed any earthly salary.

May 27

Watch the sky. My clouds reveal life. The bright clouds add beauty and life to the universe while the dark ones shed gloom but there are always periods of their separating letting My sunlight through to warm and brighten your day. I came into the world that you might have life. Remember this and walk with Me and darkness will not overtake you. Nature can reveal so much to you. The chirping birds have a cheering effect when tuned in to these sounds. Take advantage of My props in life and depression will flee from you. Rain is needed but following is a beautiful rainbow. Spring always follows winter and new life is created once again. A soul can also experience new life. My people should strive earnestly for this life.

May 28

My people need not get into a so-called "rut." I have many lifting ways, if they would only ask and believe. Praying for these lifters brings about change, and change takes the monotony out of life. Seek My spiritual gifts and an excitement can surface and bring new meaning to your daily existence. My power can add much to your limitations. Resuming your tasks can then bring you pleasure.

May 29

Inconveniences are often blessings in disguise. Offer them to Me and watch how I turn them around in your favor. Just do all you can and I will do the rest. Probabilities can turn into possibilities which can turn into miracles. I am a good God but also a jealous God. I do not want My children turning their thoughts away from Me and centering them on worldly things. Placing Me in the center glorifies Me and will do the same for you in due season. It is important for My people to make the most of their time and then relax in My love. I will furnish the strength to carry them through from day to day.

May 30

Furnish your thoughts with My scriptures. They bring healing and comfort. True meaning is transmitted to the mind while dwelling on them. The more time devoted to them, the greater the amount of understanding is revealed to you. My image will become a part of your image. The transfiguration will become gradual and recognizable by you and your acquaintances. Spiritual growth will never stop if the longing remains alive. Foster good practices.

May 31

Reenact My patience in your daily lives. Excitement can be held down to a minimum. This will keep the immune system in a healthy state. Imitate My life that I spent on earth. I hurried not. Slower, more restful movements should be practiced by all. Aiming toward maintaining your health is being obedient to My wishes. Bad personal health is often due to a person's own negligence. Your praise to Me can keep the spark ignited when health continues to be unimpaired. Age need not be a deterrent. Ask often for My strength. Then rest in My love and give it to others. Your world would stay more on an even keel if only people would abide by good practices.

JUNE

June 1

Enjoy your Freedom to worship and pray for those less fortunate who have no church to attend. So far, your country has been spared the usurping of this privilege. Pray that the blessing may continue. Consider it an honor to attend a church service and find time to worship. True worship transcends the mind and heart to Me and fulfills the purpose of your creation. I delight in My children who untiringly seek Me. They are being lead by the Spirit in all their endeavors. They need not fear for I am constantly with them. A life without fear has been tampered with from above. My grace bestowed upon you has eradicated fear. Constant prayer can keep you in this fearless state. Always remember that everything is possible with Me.

June 2

Rules abided by bring discipline to your life. Despise them not for following them enhances your character. Learn to do everything in an orderly fashion. I am a God of order and you must try earnestly to grow in My image. My rules are all laid out in My word. There can be no excuse for not knowing them. Life is enriched when you follow them. They were set down to enable you to enjoy life and live it more abundantly. Once you feel this order and fulfillment, reach out to others and help them find true blessing in life. My helping hand will help you to help others. Your servitude will be rewarded many times over.

June 3

Offer up your gardening to Me. I will bless the soil to produce beautiful flowers. The eyes of the beholders cannot help but realize a creator's power in producing such intricate beauty. Your work will display My glory. Think of this as you bend, twist and weed. The drudgery will be lifted and you will be paying homage only to Me. Your work becomes a prayer. Sowing seed and watching the growth can also be accomplished with souls. Our special deeds, remarks and actions can all be little seeds, planted in souls, which I will cultivate. Water and these souls can grow in beauty and multiply. Never underestimate the little things you do. My power turns them into greater things when offered in My name.

June 4

Anything you do for Me is credited to your heavenly account. Do not be afraid to ask for your reserve is ample. I will not cease to cater to My friends. The more you talk to Me, the more I will stay close to listen. I long for your company the same as you long for mine. No one can separate us. Your heavenly abode is being prepared. Continue to increase your work for Me. There is so much My people can do to hasten My coming. Do not keep silent when there is an opportunity to witness. I bring about certain situations to accomplish My purpose. Never stop praying in your torn world. Your prayers count so much toward the conversion of sinners. Souls must be saved and not lost. This is the reason I came into the world.

June 5

Lend an ear to the sick and lonely. They depend on My people. You are not numbered among the unfortunate but rather among the fortunate. I expect a generous heart from those that I have blessed with generosity. Assisting those in need will bear for you much fruit. Speaking words of encouragement or of My love to them can often build up their faith and hope. Many with ill health feel hopeless but you can bring them out of despondency. Make the effort and I'll supply the right words that can be spoken through you. Again, I can use you as My vessel. Shrink not from what seems like little deeds of kindness for they add up to greatness in My sight. Be a friend to all people and you will be following in My steps.

June 6

Life is but a drop of vapor compared to eternity. Nothing is sure or lasting in your life. It is only the way you live this life that earns for you My eternal life. Ask for My grace. It is a gift I bestow upon My children. This gift enables you to gain ground over the enemy. It satisfies the soul. You are able to walk in the light as I am in the light. My grace is your key to Heaven. Pray for this grace and My Father will not hold back any good thing asked for with a contrite heart. Everything is temporal in your world but in the next one it will last forever and ever.

June 7

If you desire to reminisce, think only on the good and blot out the bad. The good memories lift the spirits but the bad tear them down. Think on My life and it will invariably lift you up. Meditation has a healing effect. Steal away for quiet moments with Me and do not waste your thoughts on worldly matters. I honor and reward our quiet times. Life can be simple and not complicated as some people make it. I wait patiently for My people's attention and, when received, I pour out My own attention lavishly upon them and they become winners.

June 8

Confide in Me often as you would your best friend. This conversation is music to My ears. I wait longingly to hear your voice. Understanding this seems farfetched to some but to My dearest friends it becomes a natural process, bringing much comfort to their souls. Lingering with Me whenever possible is medicine for the spirit-man. People need all the help they can get in living out their worldly terms. Where else but from above can this help attain its fullest. Seek it at all earthly cost.

June 9

No matter your sins, My forgiveness is always available. I become saddened by them but when asked I am quick in forgiving. Do not let time elapse after committing a sin but come boldly to Me with a contrite heart. Some people feel that they have lived too wretched a life to receive forgiveness but I am a loving, forgiving God. I give My people many chances in life and wait until they come to Me using their own free will. Some miserable souls have no idea the burden that will be lifted when they repent of their sins. Hasten while there is still time for no one knows the hour of My coming or the hour of your last breath. I glorify in the satisfaction of your repentance.

June 10

My heart longs for your love. Do not deprive Me. Let us hold our secret rendezvous often, with tender conversation, strolling hand in hand. Speak to Me of your troubled heart. I can console it and mold it to perfection in spite of its flaws. Then loving Me with all your heart seals our relationship to a lasting love affair. The enemy cannot penetrate the seal for it is bound for all eternity. My people who are able to sense this reality have a joy that no one can take from them. In spite of hardships, this eternal dream is imprinted in their minds. They know that every passing day is bringing them closer to this dream. I anxiously await their return after the fulfillment of their earthly obligations.

June 11

I am in all your situations so worry not about their outcomes. Show Me your trust by changing your troubled mind. Your free will controls your mind. Prayer can help in placing interference to combat worry. Thoughts must be kept on a positive note and soon the troubled mind can be back to a peaceful state. Be on guard at all times to keep your mind free from thoughts of worldly gain. They can rob you of My joy. Be available at all times to spread My joy. Your working for Me will bring all the contentment you need in your life. Your riches will be forever to enjoy in your eternal life.

June 12

Be stable in all you do. Do not let your imagination run away with you. Think only good thoughts about your neighbor and never judge. You have no idea what that person may be going through. If his actions irritate you or seem wrong in your sight, pray for him. Do not give advice unless asked. Words can often hurt and fail to accomplish their intended purpose. My people keep rising in holiness when they put intercessory prayer into practice. This practice helps the person asking intercession to grow in character, perseverance and faith. But, best of all, it keeps the mind off of "self." At the same time, others are being helped through your prayers and, most important of all, you are acting in My divine will.

June 13

Concentrating on My love lifts you high in spirit. Worldly concerns pull one down and, the more worldly they become, the more they become trapped. Inward satisfaction can only be acquired in knowing Me, seeking Me and finding

Me. I impart the joy you need to relax in your world. Troubles will melt before your eyes. Each breath you take will create new life. I let a little of the Heavenly realm seep into your being. Earthly people cannot understand this until they experience it themselves. Pray for this invigorating feeling. It will carry you through your life untainted by the world.

June 14

Spread My love in droves upon My people. The more you give out, the more you will be given. In little loving ways speak out for My cause. Unbeknown to you, your light will shine and be visible to others. You can be the instrument for leading a person down My straight and narrow path. Release your energy and a new and more powerful energy will I implant for replacement. Remember, anything done for your brethren is done for Me also. I see all because My eye goes to and fro throughout the world. My rewards hold the only gain worth seeking. So cease not doing good.

June 15

Inaugurate strides toward eternity. New insights will be unfolded before you. The old world will take on a new transformation. I let you see it from My view. The purpose for its existence becomes a reality to you. Each one's free will will dictate how far that person will go in My Kingdom. You cannot force anyone into your way of thinking but you can lovingly point the way. Time and patience is a big factor in Christian development. Systematic reading of My word will increase your pace for growth. Pray for understanding and I will not withhold such a request. The bad get worse but I will make the good get better. My ways will become a part of your life if you open your heart to Me.

June 16

Take every disappointment in stride. Things cannot run perfectly in your world. Learn to expect this and you will stay calm. Let My love refurbish your soul. Then consign yourself over to Me for servitude. You are of great value to Me just as you are. Visualize yourself as a servant and I will build on that vision. You will be amazed at the calling I set forth through you. Temporize your actions and I will diversify them, making your life an interesting adventure. Expect My control over your life and the attainability is yours. Your comprehension in eternal matters will increase daily as long as you keep open to new thoughts and ideas. My word can be absorbed with great speed when you focus your interest on Me.

June 17

People are vindicated from their sins when they are truly sorry for them and ask My forgiveness. They must believe that I died and arose again. They should profess this often. Many a soul has been saved through this means. I expect all of My children to grow steadfast in their faith. If they sit back and do nothing, they fall by the wayside. No one knows My coming to earth but everyone should be prepared and ready. There should be a constant effort on each one's part to keep the soul spotless for My return. Render all your actions to Me and you will be credited for them. Acknowledge Me before man and I will acknowledge you before My Father in Heaven.

June 18

Your faithfulness has guaranteed you protection from above. Your investments are secured in Heaven. Even your financial status on earth works for good toward your eternal wealth. I hold no good thing back from those I want close to Me. Each step one takes toward Me is secured. Steps taken away are damaging to both soul and body. If you are walking with Me, count it all gain even though things do not look right in your sight. My ways are not your ways. So trust in your Maker and let your troubles float away like water from a duck's back. Even picture them dropping off in a large body of water and sinking, for none are lasting. Then look up. Your redemption is near.

June 19

Reach high My children. Your expectations can be granted. I am a God of love and mercy. Trust is your keyword. I will not fail you. Stamp out doubts for it hinders My work through you. A heart given to Me is a happy heart and has My sanction. It will mellow with age. It will dance right on into eternity. Self-gain is a destructive force but heavenly gain is a constructive force. Ponder on this factor. Let only good penetrate your whole being and it will vibrate to others. This becomes faith in action.

June 20

Set forth for yourself stringent rules in your prayer life and I will help you follow them. Praying while doing your dreaded tasks will help you breeze through them. The gratification you receive from it will be abounding and will derive for you lucrative rewards. Not only is self-gain achieved but great profit and blessing are also bestowed upon the recipients of your prayers. Often you can pray a person right into his or her eternal home. You may never see the results but trust that your prayers have been acknowledged beyond measure. Anxiety and fear vanish in My trusting, praying people. Do not segregate yourself from people but become involved in work to better mankind. You will learn much in the process. Life need not be a struggle but can become an adventure of great accomplishment.

June 21

Lift up your heart to heaven where it can be preserved in love. Place special emphasis on the Trinity. Venerate the cross, reviewing in your mind My passion. Worldly troubles will vanish when the true purpose in life becomes a reality. My word when ingested in faith will stir you on to new heights. The actuality of your existence will be revealed to you in tangible ways. Anyone searching will find. I will instill a thirst for spiritual knowledge. A new life will unfold taking you deeper into My truths. Your faith will grow but remember that faith without works is dead. So in your climb reach out to others and lend a helping hand.

June 22

If you have offended someone, make restitution. Then give them over to Me and keep praying for them. You will be amazed at what your prayers can accomplish. New hearts for both of you can be in the making. Patience plays a big factor. My timing does not coincide with yours. During the interim, do good for all people whom I send in your path. You are being molded so press on in spite of the odds. Temptations will come but with them I will give you strength to overcome every obstacle. You can develop a strong will and keep pressing on toward your high calling. Life becomes an exciting challenge when My rules are put into play. The more self is put into the background the more pliable you become in My hands. Offer yourself to Me for service and you will experience a great honor and privilege in serving Me.

June 23

Live one day at a time. Content yourself with the means I have afforded you. Worry not about the future and fret not about past mistakes. Take joy in the fact that I am with you always. Let your joy be noticeable to others. Your conduct can be influential to them. Develop a sensitive nature toward all. Take a genuine interest in conversations. I may use you as a vessel to deliver special words to a person. Also, listen intently as My words may come from another for you. Your spirit kept in prayer can become in tune with My spirit. Our spirits united make us one as My Father and I are one. Together, you and I stand unshakable by your world. Depend on Me for strength and it will be given you. Nothing can separate us.

June 24

Your trust in Me has brought you through many trials. Realizing My constant presence will make any future ones a simple matter. Walking your earthly life with Me immunizes you from the sting of the trials brought on by the evil one. I permit them in order to give you growth and strength and bring you closer to My heart, until our hearts beat as one. Most people who suffer call upon Me and I do answer, sometimes in ways unknown to them, but always in their favor. This unmatched way leads them toward their eternal home. Life is fleeting and will become immaterial in your eyes when you come to this realization.

June 25

Pray unceasingly. Pray that sinners be converted. Your time will thus be used wisely and your own health will improve. My word emphatically states that if you pray for others, you can be healed. My word accomplishes its purpose. No matter where you are or what you are doing, prayer can continually be offered up to God. Form such a habit for the benefits are unfathomable. You will be pleasing Me and will be right on target for your present day living. The evil one cannot gain ground with a prayer. Hence he will not stay around. An idle mind is easy prey for his works. So form the good habit of prayer and pray your way right into My Kingdom. Even your happiness in your present life can increase a hundredfold.

June 26

Look at people with the eyes of love and you will be looking out of My eyes. Love should abound while you live your earthly life. It will conquer all your battles. I am love. If you have love, I am in you and you are in Me and you can be sure of eternal life. The more you spread love, the more you are fulfilling your purpose in life. Your imitation of Me is resounding. Your good works will be blessed with an ever increasing abundance of love and grace. If one keeps giving out of love, that person will keep receiving. That is how My law of reciprocity works. Its effectiveness makes you a winner. Your belief multiplies your faith and you are in a constant growing process, drawing ever so close to My heart. Just remember, My dear, that love never fails. So keep it in use at all times and new dimensions in your life will surface to your constant amazement, thrilling your entire being.

June 27

The more righteous persons are the more noble their causes become. Their very nature can win souls for they have grown in My image. These types of people become easy to listen to because I implant My spirit to speak through them, using them as My vessel. Work toward this goal. It is a high honor. The conscience is no longer used for a target of condemnation. The spirit-man is in that higher level bringing contentment to the soul. This is the state My people should seek. It takes diligent work to arrive there but the happiness earned is well worth the price. These are My beloved working in My glory.

June 28

Condition yourself to your surroundings. Adjustments can be made easily if you accept each change as My will. Often a whole new world with opportunities galore awaits you. Instead of stumbling through from day to day, plant your feet firmly on higher ground, setting goals for yourself in My spiritual world. Helping your fellow man is a starter. Spreading kindness is a trait that is reciprocated readily. If I am called on and included in your goals, they are sanctified and receive My blessings. If you want a change but do not know which way to turn, then pray, waiting on Me for an answer. I never fail. With patience and a determination to succeed in worthwhile goals, your dreams can become realities.

June 29

Keep in mind that we do things together. The power is supplied by Me. If you actually believe this, then all things are possible for you. Renew your mind with this fact. You have a partnership that cannot fail. Introduce others to this rewarding way of living. It builds up a protective wall around you. You feel safe and secure for you have My loving arms embracing you. All fear vanishes when you are completely immersed in Me. This is experiencing My presence to the optimum. Having Me is the most security afforded you in life, sealing your future home for all eternity. When you come to this realization, a profound change takes place. Even your world takes on a more restful atmosphere. You can stay relaxed in this thought alone, bringing you a blissful peace.

June 30

Educate your spirit-man with My word. It is of utmost importance to arouse the spirit in every one of your contacts. Regulate your time and do not let the world govern it. My work on earth must be carried on by My people. It is expedient in these times to become a harvester for souls. People need direction. Be My willing instrument. Quiet times with Me will bring about a desire to serve. It is in these times that I pour My grace into you to equip you for My service. Be slow to speak, weighing your words to others so they will be acceptable to Me. I want your words to be My words. The more you commune with Me, the more you will be like Me. Cease not to call on Me and in troubled times I will carry you.

JULY

July 1

Share your spiritual gifts with others. They were given to you for that purpose. It arouses interest in a passive person. You can be the spark which can ignite in saving a new soul for Me. My gifts are many and varied. Pray to obtain them. Even one single gift throws you into a new spiritual dimension, leading you to greater holiness. Do not be afraid of the gifts. They are given for your own good as well as your fellowmen. Ask and I will not withhold such a request. In due season it will be granted. An inward spiritual longing has been planted in each and everyone. Unfortunately, some take many detours in their seeking. Others let worldly pleasure blind their eyes. I give spiritual insight to the humble who are diligently seeking. Never stop asking for more understanding, and receive My revelations in faith.

July 2

My love will sustain you from day to day. Show Me your trust by looking to Me as your source. Do not let worry or anxiety take a hold on you. Keep your mind active and pure. Stay joyful in your state of life. Wake up listening to the birds sing and take time to enjoy nature. You can ride above worldly cares. My people are crying out for help. Aid them when you can. To those that I have given much I am expecting much. Each one has been given talents to be used for My glory. Create new interests to keep the mind active. Remain joyous so others can receive the overflow. I will not let you down. Even in the midst of trials I am with you, waiting to comfort you, if only you would ask. Do not let your mind wander on earthly things but focus on Me and your eternal values. This will bring you contentment.

July 3

Do not let annoyances get you down. Your earthly life will not always run smoothly. Learn to stay calm in the midst of them. Offer them up to Me. Rebuke the devil and he will flee. Prayer is the best means to lift difficulties that assail you. You grow in grace every time that you overcome your trials. Your character is also strengthened. Surmounting one hurdle at a time is working out your salvation. Looking back and laughing at past mistakes keeps a smile on your face and a song in your heart. Praise Me for the strides you make for I am working with you and through you, helping to lead you to your eternal home.

July 4

There are so many lukewarm Christians that put the world before Me. They consider themselves righteous. Unless they turn from their ways they will not make it into My Kingdom. Their works are dead. I have tried getting their attention in many different ways. Your example and witness could be their turning point. Never underestimate your potential toward winning souls. Your years can be an asset for I have added wisdom. Just bloom where you are planted and drop little seeds along your path. I take care of the cultivation. I need many workers in My vineyard. Do not hibernate but spread yourself thin for My sake and for the sake of those around you. Be My humble ambassador with the willingness to go that extra mile.

July 5

Your enthusiasm to do My work will be rewarding. Hesitate not. The more you push ahead, the more I push for your accomplishments. I make happen what you think impossible. Every step you take I will match. At times you think I have left you but you are so wrong. It is My way of drawing you ever so close to Me. I will substantiate all your actions to the needed parties. Remember you and I are in partnership. I am one partner who will never fail you. So press on, having this great assurance. Confide in Me for all your answers and they will be given you. Our conversations will become a soothing balm to your whole being.

July 6

Your motivation comes from Me. I am the highest source, so consider yourself blessed. I increase your motivation when you act in spiritual harmony with Me. New ideas come speedily into your mind. Your Creator put them there. Follow through to the best of your ability. My power is instilled whenever needed. You can be given supernatural chores in your natural world when you keep committing yourself to Me and believe that your Creator is working through you. Let all doubts fall by the wayside. Together we stand letting the world seek its own props. Reach for the stars and do not let disappointments hinder you. You are soaking up My grace like a sponge. It is yours to keep and cannot be taken from you. Its value is priceless.

July 7

Encourage My people to read My word and familiarize themselves with a more abundant way of living. They can become more stabilized in their particular form of living. They will discover that My rules are not stringent and that, quoting My words, they can counterattack the evil one who prowls around seeking someone to devour. His attacks come by way of the mind. My word is sharper than any sword so use it often to win your battles during your earthly life. Unlearned people do not understand how to cope with negative thoughts and fall under such pressure. Pray that you may receive spiritual enlightenment and in turn help to enlighten others. My ministers are few and the big job of evangelizing must be shouldered by My faithful followers. It will turn your own life around and bless you richly,

July 8

When one gives his life completely over to Me, repents of his sins, and accepts Me as Lord and Savior, he is baptized in the Spirit. Life then takes on a new dimension. You feel new life in your inner most being. This joy you receive comes from above. My Spirit gifts are poured out for My followers to receive. Accept them in faith and ask for My power to exercise them. Have patience with those around you who do not understand and comprehend My Spirit gifts. The scales will be lifted from their eyes in due season. Much prayer and sacrifice on my followers' parts can speed the infilling of My Spirit in others. My Spirit gifts are given freely to those who ask and are open and ready. Keep in prayer for this indwelling. One knows when one receives for the joy is unimaginable. That person experiences our oneness. A thirst for spiritual knowledge ensues and new growth begins.

July 9

Let your faith be your controlling factor. Believe in the positive realm and your thinking will stay in that plane. Let My joy radiate from you and spill over into others. Having My Spirit in you is all that you need for I am all in all. Realize your good fortune and determine to bring others to your good fate by sharing your knowledge. Words spoken for My cause will be backed with My power. Faith is one's greatest asset when it is God oriented. My dwelling in you leads you to new heights. Your latter years need not be dull. Reach out to others and My life in you will keep you vibrant. Selfishness will gradually disappear. My nature and your nature will merge. When an unforeseen mishap occurs, pick yourself up as I did My cross and follow Me. The cross leads to your crown.

July 10

Slow down in your fast-paced world. Enjoyment is only felt in ease of movement. Let your energy last throughout the day. Sweet rest is given at night to take you through to another day. Overexertion can play havoc with the body. Remember your body is the Temple of My Spirit. Keep it in good working condition. Prayer and meditation add new life to the body so exercise these practices often. A healthy mind and body can withstand the pressures of life. Everyone must toil for a daily living and take stock of the methods to those ends. Learning to walk and talk with Me brings about your right answers personified. Living a good, honest and holy life brings about the sweet rest needed. When sin weighs one down, rest does not come easily. This is why I stress "repent" in My word. My ways are the best so learn of Me and keep yourself healthy and happy.

July 11

God knows what is best for you. Repeat this line often and pray to realize this fact. Relax in My love and accept circumstances as My will, especially after you have prayed about the matter. I set things right in My way and timing. Trust and believe are your keys to use often to live life more freely. The more you use these keys, the lighter the load becomes. You can transform troubles into grace. Good can come out of bad situations when I am called upon. Daily ask for My intervention and I will not fail you.

July 12

Keep growing spiritually and you will be able to experience some of My Kingdom on your earth. There is much to learn from My word, from people I place in your path and from books whose authors have reached My higher realm. Pray for enlightenment and the power of discernment, so that you can sort out the true from the false doctrine. This quality is one of My gifts of the Spirit. Growing in knowledge keeps the mind's gears in operation. An idle mind loses its functional capabilities. Growing spiritually helps one cope with one's natural environment. The purpose for one's creation thus has more meaning and can be acted out to the fullest. With spiritual knowledge the mind is able to control the body and operate the body at a more normal level, thus keeping it healthy.

July 13

My love for each and everyone is greater than any earthly love. I long for their reciprocation. Once My Spirit dwells in a person, that person becomes changed in his innermost being. If only people would ask for this indwelling. Living life in one's own power never brings true happiness. I supply your needs in spite of your worldly cares. My grace will take you over the highest mountain tops and lift you out of the deepest valleys. I bestow this on My faithful followers free and without being asked. If only people would accept Me as their closest friend, I would lavish them with My gifts, especially those that will lead them to their eternal reward with Me. Once they encounter My love, they cannot contain it. They end up giving to others and I keep them replenished. Never stop telling the world of My love. The evil one works overtime in the world and people are devoured through his deception.

July 14

The highest elevation of success is the allowance of the Holy Spirit to dwell within. The realization of His presence is heart warming. A soothing effect permeates your entire being when He is knowingly present and acknowledged. Coordinate with Him in your decision making. You will aspire to greater spiritual heights in your present world. This is due to the fact that His spirit and your spirit have merged into one. It is hard for the finite mind to comprehend but accepting it all in faith is the answer. Then question not and your faith can be built up to overflowing proportions. Treasure your faith. It is a gift of insurmountable value.

July 15

Try to measure up to My standards which are spelled out for you in My word. Steal time from your busy day to read My book of great price. Ask for the mind's enlightenment and it shall be given to you. Your pure intentions will be honored. Your life can remain stable and on a more even keel. People cause their own fluctuations by lack of knowledge. Help yourself to live a stable life in an unstable world. Pray to obtain the qualities needed for a life leading to spiritual perfection. Your days will not be wasted and regrets will no longer exist. Your footing will hold and will withstand the storms for you will become a rock.

July 16

I am infilling you with My strength. Bask in it. Release your loved ones to Me. Concern yourself not with what you see. The benefits derived from the unseen far outweigh what your mind comprehends. I was a human sacrifice for all mankind. My sufferings were not understood by human eyes that watched. Trust Me. Lean on Me and not your own understanding. Human sufferings offered to Me in faith release souls. Seek understanding and glimpses of it will be revealed to you. Love My people with sacrificial love and you will keep growing in My image.

July 17

Your loved one is receiving the much rest needed. Rely on My judgment. He is being sanctified. I will let him see beyond. His future is secured. My own are gathered up in tender mercy. They shall mount up as eagles and reach great heights unknown to man. Save your pity for the poor souls that shun Me. Be eager to push on for My cause. My light will shine brighter to you in your darkened world. Your faith deepens with every passing moment you spend with Me.

July 18

Look forward to each new day with eager anticipation. Expect My interventions and accept them. I am there to comfort you and wipe away your tears. My church is My sheepfold and I am the good shepherd. With tender compassion I gather My sheep together and comfort them. Rest in this fact and let your worries melt. The more you believe My word, the more you will grow in faith and the cares of this world will seem to loose their grip on you. Until you relax in My love you will not enjoy completely the abundant life I have freely given you. Be cognizant of this and work at obtaining full enjoyment from day to day.

July 19

I have given each one a measure of faith. The increase is dependent largely upon you. Venture out among My people exploiting this faith and you will not only keep yours growing but will increase that of others. No matter how small your deeds, they are acted upon and honored. My Father sees all. Keep this in mind and make every effort to please Him. Look forward to the great reunion day when the saints of God will be gathered up. See yourself numbered among them.

July 20

Your cry for help is not left unheard. Often I send My ministering angels to help you out of your dilemmas and comfort you. My people seem to take the good for granted and only remember the bad. Reverse this process and joy will penetrate your being. Keep a smile on your face to help lift up those in despair. Ask for My mighty power to draw people to you. Then with this power lift them up to Me. Making a habit of this practice will bring you much joy. Anything done for My people is paid back to you many times. So reach out to My starving, hurting people and your own troubles will melt away. Your time will fly by quickly while I am preparing your eternal home. You cannot fathom the beauty I have awaiting you. Rest in this thought.

July 21

Learn to recognize My spirit working in you and through you. Cooperate with My promptings. The call yesterday to your Christian friend, whom you had not seen for some time, was prompted by Me. I placed the words in your mouth for her comfort. I work in mysterious ways. Cultivate your desire for service. Your life will develop true meaning and purpose. My word can help substantiate your actions. I have vindicated you of past sins and clothed you in righteousness. Your ways are becoming My ways. Do not hesitate to intervene in situations where My people need answers for you are My servant and My helper. Keep emerged in prayer so the evil one cannot gain entrance.

July 22

Whenever you pray, resign yourself to the fact that My will will be done. I listen to your pleas. I honor your prayers even though you do not see the results. Your gratification will all be supplied when you enter eternal life. Your "thank you's" will never cease. I am the only source of your existence so do not let any blockage exist. Go not by what you see but keep walking in faith. The more you believe, the more I will reveal. The infinite will be felt in your being. The heart in man is My Tabernacle. Keep it spotless. Renew your mind with My word every chance you get. Your body can begin to become glorified before reaching Heaven. Joy and happiness are two qualities I am pleased to administer to My loving people on earth. Count yourself blessed beyond measure.

July 23

Subsidize your good fortune by giving freely. My eye sees all. Too many people are in need. Be adamant in your giving. Go that extra mile to help friends and even strangers. Measure up to My standards by giving and your supply will not run out. This is trusting your creator to the fullest. The mind will shift to others and a healing of self is brought about by Me. Never grow tired of doing good. Your Heavenly Father sees all and is a rewarder. He transforms the heart. Set your goals high and He will help you obtain them. His word will not fail you so learn of His promises. Keep a song in your heart and let it ring out as praise to the Lord. You are not insignificant but very precious in the eyes of your creator.

July 24

If you have bodily ills, do not hesitate to call on long-standing church members to pray over you and anoint you with oil. I release My power through certain anointed vessels and allow healings to take place. Some are instant and some come about slowly. My Eucharist is also a healing contact. Receive Me in faith often. The results can be amazing to My believers. Knowing that My will can be accomplished in you and through you should spur you on for My greater works in your earthly life. I am the same yesterday, today, and always. Committing yourself to Me is a prime requisite for My service. Keep yourself holy and pure and you will become an open channel for My mighty power to flow through. I work in unusual ways and circumstances but all for the good of My people. An open thanksgiving and testimony is important for it displays My glory. Faith can be built up in those who lend Me an ear. All My workings are for good. Just believe.

July 25

Be gentle in speech at all times. The tone of voice can be cutting and hurt someone deeply. It is better to remain silent than to show irritation in your voice. Develop My spirit and the atmosphere will remain pleasant. You set the stage for priestly living. Determine in your heart to remain docile and let no anger surface. The disposition is controlled in the heart. Work at diligently following in My footsteps, calling on

Me for help. A serene countenance will ensue and your health will thrive. Practice can bring about perfection. Talking with Me about troubling situations relieves your tension within and has therapeutic effects. I am your answer.

July 26

Mingle among My people and I will supply you with the words needed for their ears. They all have struggles to surmount. Unbeknown to you, you can be the overcoming force. I work in a quiet gentle way, only nudging, and let My followers energize their free will in carrying it out. If they adhere to this, I supply them with My gift of knowledge. My servants receive so much for the efforts they put forth. In these last days, I need many more soldiers to recruit in My army to go into battle for My cause. One need only commit himself to Me and I bring about the changes needed for My service and all will be for his betterment. The transformation in one's character is indescribable.

July 27

When troubling matters seem to oppress you, quote scriptures from My word. They are called the sword of the spirit. Every thrust of the sword pushes the enemy away. Having My word in your memory gives you protection in times needed. So memorize My word for such times. Oppression can be lifted, as you have discovered. Pass this on to others. The more scripture is memorized, the more weapons one has in his possession. After their use, a comfort is felt in your spirit. You have used My word in times of trouble and sickness and found it can lift the symptoms of disease. The evil one can be pushed back in his tracks. When this method is applied, My people can bring peace to their spirit and their world of turmoil can become less devastating.

July 28

Share with others the gifts I have bestowed upon you. Share your knowledge of Me and My great love. Share your material blessings. Hoarding is despicable in My sight. I gave Myself on the cross so all could be entitled to eternal life. Your giving out of love is your great commission on earth and will lead you to your sanctification. Giving your time to pray for others lifts you in My spiritual realm. Share your spiritual experiences with friends and neighbors and they, in turn, will open up to you. Together you will have common holy ground to expound on. This interest is of a high nature and can have a lifting effect on your whole being. You will begin to hunger for these talks and gossip about neighbor will no longer have precedence. Pray for My nature and your popularity among My people will increase at a fast pace. In these last days My people are seeking answers.

July 29

Measure up to My expectations, those of knowing, loving, and serving Me. Learn of Me and I will make your heart like mine. You learn more of Me every time you read My word. Love Me with all your heart and with no strings attached. I will honor your love by increasing your capacity to love. Be ever ready to serve Me. Practice on My people. Whatever you do for them, you are doing for Me. See Me in them. Your grace will abound as you apply this practice to your daily living. As you continue to grow in Me and I in you, your ecstasy of just knowing this truth will cause you to rejoice with your whole being. The gift of My power will I bestow on My faithful ones so do not be surprised when an impossible deed is accomplished through you. These last days are exciting ones. Stay close to Me.

July 30

Migrate into My spiritual realm and get rest for your soul. Your breathing will become deeper and your tense muscles will loosen. Stay in this state and relax with Me. Talk with Me or meditate on Me. The results will renew your strength. If you make work of our visits, you have not completely released self. I want all of you for many moments throughout the day. Search your heart and search My heart and let us merge them into one. The beat will be in perfect rhythm. Your journey in life is enhanced with each heartbeat.

July 31

Count your blessings often to keep your spirit high. Visiting the sick and the less fortunate can be eye-openers. Remember your purpose in life and do not seek self-satisfaction. While earning your way into My Kingdom, gather up others along your way. Making this progress can bring joy to your heart. Work diligently among My people and you will not lack wisdom. I increase My gifts in My productive ones. If you are among the disabled, then offering up your disability can be beneficial in overcoming obstacles in your life. Let love dominate your being. Never feel sorry for yourself as oppression takes over and you are caught in the snare of the evil one. Let My word guide you along the open path leading to My Kingdom. Your willingness can be fortified with prayer.

AUGUST

August 1

My angels are My helpers. In time of protection, call upon them. I often send them to you, unknown by you. Develop an awareness of their presence. They avert accidents and push away death from your doorstep. Sometimes I need to send legions of them to fight the enemies in a spiritual battle. Each person has a special guardian angel whom they should acknowledge. My people have no idea of the activity going on in the spiritual world. I have given visions of angels to some of My elect. This experience is overwhelming and heart warming. Surrender yourself to Me and call upon My angels and you will not be denied. My angels are constantly busy in these last days with the enemy and their followers in their last sprints. My day of return is not far off. This is harvest time.

August 2

Have empathy for My people. Judge not their motives. They may have been directed by Me. You will be judging Me. Learn silence and do not be quick to express opinions. Listen and you will not only learn but self will be put in the background where it belongs. Socialize with good Christian friends and direct the conversation on spiritual matters. It will inspire your spirit and attract your interest. Conversation on material things is fleeting and does nothing for your spirit. Following My guidelines will win good friends and help for gracious living.

August 3

Seize every chance you get to expand your knowledge on spiritual matters. Your gift of discernment can sort out what is not of Me. Be not biased but open to hearing truths. Praise with My people for I dwell among their praises. Wherever people are gathered in My name, I am performing miracles. There is a new wave of interest in people seeking rest for their unrest. Others attend meetings only out of curiosity. Whatever the motive, I am walking among the people as I did 2,000 years ago. It is so simple to reach Me after My people give their hearts over to Me. Many have done so and the result is in their favor. Those who do not have a grave future ahead. You who are aware of a coming holocaust are to sound a warning to the less fortunate. Care not what people think but care for their eternal safety.

August 4

Suppress anger before it is allowed to surface. Prayer is the best means. Ask God for help. In anger, you are only giving in to the devil and letting him control you. Reverse this process immediately, showing him that you want no part of his control on your life. When he sees his tempting is useless, he will flee. It is when you succumb that he stays with you. Reciting scripture is another means to fight off these attacks. Anger also plays havoc with your health. Confess this sin instantly, asking forgiveness, and with effort on your part it shall be granted. A clear conscience can develop in My people which can lead them to become perfect as I am perfect.

August 5

My child, humble yourself at all times for without Me you are nothing. Keep your mind fixed on Me and your nothingness becomes transformed. Breathe in My peace with every breath you take. Think only on the things above where the value is everlasting. Earth cares should not take precedence. Much anguish can be avoided if my people heed what I am telling them. The evil one flees when he cannot distract the mind. He would like to get your mind troubled. If he can plant a few earthly thoughts he is happy, especially if he can get your concentration on them, thus playing cards with him. Center your attention on Me and see the good it brings. Continue to pray for conversions and make a game out of praying for strangers you see. Your every prayer is honored. On the great judgment day you will see your prayer accomplishments.

August 6

Eternal life should be the Number 1 aim in every person's life. Those who feel they have obtained it and are in My perfect will have a duty to win others to this life. Their exuberance will reflect My love and thus draw the attention of others. The world is crying out for love and, until My people experience this love, they will only keep groping in the dark. I am the light that opens the eyes to faith-sight. When My word penetrates their minds, a hope springs into their being. They realize they are not living in vain. This realization brings about a desire to love. And love for your fellowmen is the image I portrayed for you on earth, climaxing it for all of you with My sacrifice at Calvary. Your ever increasing love should spur you on to the sacrifice of winning souls for Me.

August 7

Accept the mysteries of life in simple faith. The finite mind is not capable of comprehending all the spiritual aspects. Believing without seeing is great faith and will be honored by My Father in Heaven. My word is sufficient. If people would take time to study it, they could untangle their complicated lives and find it easy to live one day at a time applying My principles. Ask for My power, which takes you beyond your capabilities, and it will be afforded you. Remember to give Me your troubles and then act as if they do not exist. They will become minimized and some will even disappear. Keep Me in the center of your life at all times.

August 8

Your salvation has already been accomplished, ascribed to My death on the cross. Relax in this fact and stay pure and holy to obtain it. Without My sacrifice all people would perish. Because of My devout love for each and everyone, I made the sacrificial offering and bore pain that no human being could endure. Those who sin thwart My intention and lose what I gained for them. If only they would ask forgiveness, I would turn their whole lives around. I will only enter souls by invitation and they must be of a penitent heart. My friends linger with Me in long conversations. This becomes rewarding for both of us. Shun worldly distractions and cling to divine matters. It will profit you greatly.

August 9

Seek not the things of this world but seek those you can help in this world. People need to hear and understand My word. Often a friend or even a stranger can set the spark for a spiritual growth. Each one in My creation is so different but each has been equipped with the same measure of faith. It is up to the individual to develop it. Too many fall by the wayside. You may be just the one to pick them up with a kind word or deed. Never stop going out of your way to lend a helping hand. Push the things of this world out of the way so there is no hindrance in pressing on for My cause. My blessing is upon such a person. Remember life is so short and worldly things cannot be added to your credit, but spiritual endeavors will add numerous gems to the crown which is being prepared for you in heaven.

August 10

Turning your loved one over to Me releases your hold and puts his best interests in My hands. You are set free of worry and your trust in Me is honored. Often your hold hampers a person. When that person is free from earthly ties, I work freely on his behalf. My ways are so different than yours. The soul is so much more important than the body. My timing is not according to yours but there again I know what is best. I am their Heavenly Father. I have a greater love for My children than any earthly father. Muster up courage to place a loved one completely in My hands and rest assured that the right thing will be accomplished in his behalf. Prayer reinforces My actions.

August 11

Do not plan ahead for future events and you will not be disappointed. Instead, take each day as it comes with its joys and its sorrows. You can always make it through one day. Live that day for Me. There will be no regrets. I can turn your sorrows into blessings and add grace besides. You will be learning to live life the way I intended it to be lived. Anxiety will play no part in your life. Too many people tell Me how to run their life instead of trusting and accepting My will. They have not the slightest idea of the motives behind My will for them. Often they thwart the blessing intended for them. Seek only My will. Sit back and collect your blessings.

Your life will take on new turns that you never dreamed possible.

August 12

I can recreate in all My people a new life. Ask with a contrite heart. Draw ever so close to Me and I will draw ever so close to you. Depend on Me for everything and give thanks for all as I work in the good and bad situations for your own good. I can sanctify your soul when you place complete trust in Me. All your works should be for the good of mankind. My life exemplified this fact. Do likewise and your glory will be felt in your innermost being. I am true to My word so study it for your consolation. Peace in your life is attainable. Strive for it.

August 13

Since you have made Me your home, wherever you go in your travels you are right at home. Looking up a church with My body of believers makes your worship a double blessing. You have learned deep in your spirit that I am with you always and will never leave you. People single you out for your nature is becoming more like mine. Your smile is becoming warm. I, your God, am speaking to you. Be ever attentive to My words. They are to be used to benefit others. Hesitate not to relay My messages. Some may ridicule you but their blind eyes have not been opened to the truth. I will bless a number of people through your faithfulness.

August 14

You wonder why your loved one is still suffering. Your prayers and others have benefited him greatly. The good he is doing lying there helpless is insurmountable. His patient endurance is saving many souls. Many of My saints were unknown on earth but are acknowledged to the fullest in My kingdom. Worldly renown is not acknowledged here in heaven. Your loved one's favor is growing moment by moment. He is not being neglected but only being glorified. If you knew his glory to come you would be celebrating.

August 15

Develop a compassion for My people. A cold heart can mellow with practice. A "caring" leads to sharing. If you give I will keep increasing your abundance in those areas. Having compassion increases the capacity to love. Your love can make a difference in lives you touch in your cold world. Everyone needs a lift. If you can be an instrument in lifting up My people, you will be lifted to greater heights in My Kingdom. Your personality will take on a depth that draws people to you. My people are winners. Their spirit keeps growing and never dies. Their life is worth living.

August 16

When life's problems wear you down, come to Me for strength. Sit quietly with your mind on Me and I will renew your strength. Often the things you fret about do not come to pass. There is no need to work yourself up with imagined circumstances. Instead, give the troubled thoughts to Me. I replace them with peace. Life is pretty much what you make it. You are the controller. Yes, there is even peace in the midst of storms when I am included. I can turn the sails and set you on the proper course. If you believe and trust and practice patience, you can endure all trials of life with ease. The mind controls all the bodily functions. So stay healthy dwelling on positive, pure thoughts. Erase bad, negative thoughts from your mind by refusing to dwell on them. You can thus stay in My will and be exonerated.

August 17

Take my hand and we will trod the path of life together. Practice My presence whether in silence or in conversation. I will take the sting out of life. Loneliness will not take occupancy for I fill that gap. The evil one flees when you take no part in the negative thoughts he tries to force into your mind. Praying without ceasing keeps him from making an entrance. I delight in My children's company and lend an ear to what they say. Even their thoughts are known to Me. Nothing can be hidden from Me. Determine to stay close to Me and the protection of My angels will be granted on your request. Keep picturing Me with My arms outstretched and I will cradle you with My love.

August 18

My spirit dictates to your spirit and the results have been your messages. With your acting upon this, numerous people are reaping the benefits. If My people would become doers of the word, the beneficial results would be astounding. My people think they have not the talents for My service. They fail to realize that I supply the talent, know-how and power. They should sever the relationships that lead away from spirituality and develop new ones that enhance our relationship. The spirit in them will want to keep growing and they will take measures to do so. The efforts My people put forth will be enriched by Me. Try to be the one to keep pointing new people in My direction. They, in turn, can do likewise. The lost can be found by applying this "snowball" effort.

August 19

Keep in prayer and no evil will overtake you. Restrict yourself to a disciplined life. It is so easy for the world to take one over that it is necessary to constantly be on guard. Sow good seed day by day so you can reap the harvest. Prepare your way as well as those of others. Make Me well pleased in all you do. Work from a strategic standpoint to make your time count toward your eternal destiny. Material worries should be eliminated. They wear you down and make you lose countless blessings. I long to serve My people but unfortunately they have little time for Me. There are tremendous tasks to be performed and so few to accomplish them. Say you will be mine to use and glory will surround you. Humble yourself in My sight and you will be exalted. My words will not fail you.

August 20

Rest and immerse yourself in My love. The body needs release from tension. This is obtained in quiet meditation with your mind staid on Me. The world's pace is too fast. Come to Me for rest. Know your limits and do not push beyond or a breakdown of the body occurs. After your short meditations with Me you can resume your work with added strength. You were made to walk and talk with Me and doing so keeps the body flowing in a more normal manner. Besides doing what pleases Me you are adding blessings upon yourself. I did not hurry when I walked the earth. A hurried mind is not one of peace. If My people obtain this peace, they have learned many spiritual lessons. They have surrendered themselves to Me. Moderate all you do to keep at a normal pace and you will measure up to My expectations.

August 21

I will satisfy all your longings. Release yourself to Me. Let Me hear your petitions from your mouth for I long to hear your voice. Be specific on your wants and I will satisfy them in ways that are best for you. Give thanks to Me even before your prayers are answered to show Me your faith. Your child-like faith will be honored. Be ever grateful for past favors. Count them from time to time to evaluate My goodness. Your innermost being, the heart, is our secret dwelling place. Enter often for consolation. It is this meeting place where our friendship is restored. Your vitality will stem from such meetings and your spiritual renewal will prosper.

August 22

Stir up your emotions with My love and they will be kept under control at all times. Temper is the uncontrollable emotion that sprouts from the evil one. His place can take roots in you if allowed. Be on guard at all times to avoid emotional upsets and will to do so. Calling on Me for help will bring instant relief. Consistent practice will soon eliminate the temper habit. Whatever you find helpful in your spiritual walk should be shared with others. This reinforces your own stability. Giving out to others in such a way blesses you tenfold and increases your spiritual growth.

August 23

Systematize your work and it will become acceptable in My sight. Rules must be made for oneself to follow as much as those made for the good of all. A transfiguration can take place within that is pleasing to oneself. These jubilees within inspire one to a higher plain of living. The stimulation furnished by Me enhances your life and drudgery is removed. Joy replaces sorrow as the spirit-man surfaces. A feeling of self-satisfaction can emerge and can keep growing if watered at My spiritual well which never runs dry.

August 24

Praying for My people is being a servant for Me. Your prayers help them tremendously. At times you may feel useless but you always have the capability to pray. Forming the habit of praying for others brings untold blessings upon you and benefits you by keeping your mind active. My love is manifested in you when your mind is centered on the well-being of others. Praying for others minimizes the perplexities in your own life. Any sacrifices you make for others is a form of prayer. Offer up all your services for the benefit of mankind. This alone lifts the burden for your works are not in vain.

August 25

The start of a successful spiritual life is praise. It lifts the heart and mind to Me. The most natural way is in song. Let it ring out from your innermost being. Your spirit is renewed and an invigorating effect is felt in your whole being. I delight in your praises whether they be in song, speech or thought. I become raptured in them and impregnate My joy in you. The more you praise, the happier you become. Your faith grows with spiritual contact. The more your faith grows, the easier it is to cope with worldly problems. Your praises can compensate for past mistakes. Worthy is the lamb that was slain for your sake.

August 26

Tread through the storms of life with complete confidence in Me, your Savior. I paid for your salvation so believe and follow My pattern for your life. Any problems in your life are trivial in view of the life to come. Do not pity people in distress for their destiny may be great in My sight. Some things in your life are not understandable by the human mind. If you want to see beyond your human sight, then keep building up your faith and walk steadfastly to the finish line and question not the circumstance. Live by My rules in spite of the outcome. The ease of conscience is worth the cost.

August 27

Commit your ways to Me. They will have My blessings upon them. Then, whatever the outcome, you will know it is My will. My sanction will be upon all you do. Greatness in this life should hold little meaning. Your greatness in My Kingdom will be measured by your good deeds. Make them many, no matter how small. Offer up all your menial tasks to Me. I have a way of turning them into blessings. Submit your entire being to Me and your measurement of accomplishment will far exceed your expectations. Meeting My standards will win unlimited grace.

August 28

You ask for favors but how about asking to be in My favor. Your blessings are then poured out in abundance. Attacks from the evil one prompts counterattacks by My angels. Being on My side keeps Me ever at your side. I am your way. If you could only believe this, the battle in life would be over before it could even begin. Use My available tools to learn of Me and then follow in My footsteps. Your works will be great in My sight. No attempts by those formed against you will succeed. Your Master keeps watch over you day and night so fear need not exist. My people remain winners in their world as well as the next.

August 29

You are consumed in the fire of My love. Knowing this fact deep in your spirit makes it possible to face the challenges in life unafraid. My children who follow My statutes feel this protection. They flounder not in the dark for they sense My light. I delight in the observance of continual spiritual growth of My children, but am also saddened for those who remain stagnant. Your accumulated knowledge coupled with My inspiration can transpire you to new heights unknown by man. Push forward with the determination to overcome shortcomings. Age has no barrier when the spirit-man rises within. This lifting action will keep you going from glory to glory.

August 30

Be humble and keep pride in the background. I can then best mold you in My image. When with a penitent heart you ask Me for help, I chip away ever so gently at your faults, thus shaping you into a more perfect vessel. Be not disheartened when things go wrong, but count it as your molding process. Character is built up over a period of years. Take inventory and dispel bad habits before they take root. Try to develop a quiet nature. All forms of gossip must be eliminated before it tears down My loved ones I created. Praying for others will build them up and you as well. My people should aim for constant growth.

August 31

Let love permeate your whole being. A selfish nature cannot exist in a love atmosphere. A love nature has a soothing effect on all your contacts. It is refreshing to your own soul. Spread this love to the unlovable. They desperately need it. Your measure of return will be a hundredfold. Remember I am walking along side you watching every little kind act you perform. It is recorded in My Book of Life which will be opened up on your day of judgment. What a happy reunion day My people will experience who let love dominate in their lives. If you feel incapable of loving, pray and ask for an infilling of this love nature and then work at the development of it. You will soon find that you have an ample supply to give away. A tender heart will emerge.

SEPTEMBER

September 1

All things are possible for those who believe. Your dreams can become realities. Ask and, if it be My will, I will give you the desires of your heart. Often, with patience and endurance, the dream begins to take shape. I mold My children for My greater works. Unless they go through a training period, they are not prepared to handle their request. My timing is My will for you, so wait for Me. Always do the best you can on any job set before you and I will freely give when the time is ripe. Since you are My child, rest in the thought that I will never leave you or forsake you. This should bring contentment in spite of your day by day struggles.

September 2

I have given everyone special talents. They must be worked upon and developed and acknowledged as My gifts. I add to or take from depending on their use. To those who are given much, much is required. Take inventory of your talents and their use. Using them for the good of My people is commended by Me but using them for personal gain I frown upon. Ponder upon this and make changes necessary to please Me. You will be surprised at the outcome. Anything done in My name receives My sanction and blessing. Give the glory to Me and there will be no end to where I will take you.

September 3

Stay compatible with My will. Resignation brings an ease in living. Learn to recognize My voice and My guidance. Discuss your problems with Me. The mere mention often brings about the solution or dissolution of problems and, in other cases, at least the strength to bear them. Keep in mind that this life offers you the opportunity to earn your way to great heights in My Kingdom. This thought alone should help you bear your burdens and lessen the load. No matter how rough the road, you can keep going with My help. Your graduation day will be one of great celebration in My Kingdom. In summation, it will be worth it all when you see Me.

September 4

Let not your heart be troubled. Render it all to Me. The consummation of My love is at your disposal. Let yourself be saturated with it. As long as the evil one prowls the earth there will be troubles but those who walk close to Me will receive grace to sustain them. I can turn your trials into blessings that will count toward your eternal reward. Your setbacks in your world are your stepping stones to eternal life. Be not discouraged or envious of your neighbor. Your time of jubilee will soon be at hand. In My world there will be total rejoicing. This thought alone should keep you content and happy until My return.

September 5

Be a witness for Me and hesitate not to speak up for My name's sake. Your acquired knowledge can win souls. You can create new hearts in others. I will place the words in your mouth. The more you give out, the faster My spirit will reveal new truths to you. Reading My word will open your mind to new realities. Keep your ears open in sharing sessions. When the mind is open to My truth, I fill it and give you the gift of discernment. With your mind ever fixed on Me, your bodily functions flow in a more normal fashion. Disease can be averted. So let your time be spent in an ever growing process.

September 6

My heart aches for My people. They need Me but will not take the measures to find Me. I wait to enter their hearts by invitation. Oh, how much more meaning their life would have if only they accepted Me as their Lord and Savior. Be My ambassador and point these lost souls in a subtle, gentle manner. A few soft-spoken words about My goodness can be a seed planted. Your works will be acknowledged and multiplied by Me and I will take care of the cultivation of that seed. Your compassion should lead to a boldness to save My people from the fate they will soon face. You may be the only key available to a person's eternal life. Be generous in unlocking doors for My sake. Your blessings will be calculated and win for you untold favors.

September 7

Release all your possessions to Me, even your loved ones. I can then work freely on your behalf, doing what is best for all concerned. I honor your complete trust, even to the extent of performing miracles on your behalf. You hold the controlling key which is that of complete trust. Learn to give it all to Me and changes you never dreamed possible will occur, including your health. Your words to Me must be deep, heartfelt words and not hollow words. I am able to differentiate for I read the heart. My people should turn their lives around before it is too late. Now is the moment, while words can still penetrate the heart. Some hearts become so hard that they turn to stone. No one knows the time or the hour of My impending return. They must heed My warning.

September 8

Step out in faith for Me and I will meet that step with a capability that will surprise you. Strengthen your faith with My word and things you thought impossible will become possible. My rewards are not only for the next world. I delight in watching you grow spiritually and add talent where needed to spread My word. You are My church and growth is vitally important in these last days. My Son's death must be understood and accepted by everyone that they gain their salvation. Be My instrument to open the deaf ears. I need you the same as you need Me. Your preparation for My impending return will be anointed by Me with added ability to gather others along the way.

September 9

If My people would humble themselves, I would exalt them in due season. They should keep in mind that every good gift comes from Me. I look for thankfulness. I can snatch away at any time. Often I do so to teach a lesson. When you have setbacks, be not disheartened but keep pressing on to your high calling. I will guide you in all your ways and will instill understanding. My righteous have My protection, but woe to those who are not under My protection. Pray to keep in My grace lest you fall. Renew your baptismal promises and the Holy Spirit will infiltrate your being. Your mind will become stigmatized with righteousness. The evil one will not be able to penetrate such a stabilized state of being.

September 10

Recognizing My presence at all times brings a gratification to the soul. Learning to trust Me and relying on My protection helps one tremendously to cope with obstacles. The peace which I dower out to My own people refurbishes their entire being. Joy is the outcome and is noticeable by others. My children are not left orphans when they reach out to Me. Unfortunately too many do not realize what I have to offer. Pride holds them back from asking. Their doubts have kept their faith from growing. Life has so much more to offer with Me in the center. Try to convey this message to the less fortunate and your joy will be multiplied.

September 11

Quiet your mind with thoughts on your world to come. What has already occurred is past history and cannot be changed so do not dwell on it. The evil one will bring troubling thoughts to your mind and only you can erase them with the will to do so. Speak not about them for it only opens the wound. Learn to rise above all problems and your character will be enhanced. Praying for others is a quick relief for your own situation and will take the mind off yourself. Associate with Christian friends, those that have the tendency to pick you up. Allow laughter to ring out for it is medicine to the soul. Go to My word often for guidance. Let your life be a challenge and do not settle for a dull daily existence. Even the dullness of your daily chores can be lifted when I have been invited in. Keep learning of Me and become more like Me. This is My will for you.

September 12

I give according to the measure you give out. Giving nothing leaves your life at a standstill for I have nothing to work with to multiply. Your time, money, prayers and sacrifices offered in My behalf and for My people count toward a richer life for you filled with My grace and blessing. I see all and know all the motives of your heart. There is nothing that can be hidden from Me. I know your capabilities and your limitations and delight in adding to them. So reach out and take the first step and I will meet each one. My word will not fail you. Read it often for assurance and consolation. Remember you are not alone. I am always with you.

September 13

Wherever My people go, I go with them and keep loving them. Even though I may dislike some things they do, I never stop loving them. This is why I wish so desperately that none shall perish. I long so much to help each and everyone but wait until asked. If then your wishes are not granted, despair not. I have your well-being under supernatural control. Believe this and disappointment will not be your lot. Keep striving for your high calling and soon we will meet where there will be no more tears, only complete unending happiness .

September 14

Rest in the fullness of My love and captivate the ecstasy. Minor irritations will fade away. While you are resting, I will cleanse you with purified water from above. You will sense this action and feel the joy it imparts. Let My love flow through you into others. The magnifying effect will spread throughout your daily contacts. An enrichment of the soul will manifest itself. This enrichment is your reward for your faithfulness. My tenderness becomes yours through our day to day conversations. Signs that seem insignificant to some become our point of contact. Our relationship will keep growing because you will not allow a hindrance. There is no measurement to the favors I will bestow on you. Your light will shine in your dark world, illuminating the paths for others.

September 15

Live for others and not for yourself. Turn yourself outward instead of inward. There are many hurting people wearing masks. Kindness can go a long way in reaching out to My people. Often you can set the tone for their day, whether it be a high one or low one. Put on a happy face each day to lift the downtrodden and you will develop a happy nature. This is one of My blessings for giving. A visit to the sick will have you counting your blessings. Time spent reaching out to My people is time well spent and will all be written down in My Book of Life to be opened up on your judgment day.

September 16

Do not ignore Me by shunning My presence. I am with you at all times. I glory in your praises and long to converse with you. Form a picture of Me and keep it ever before you. Acknowledging Me keeps you acknowledged before My Father in Heaven. Discuss your problems with Me, leave them with Me and trust Me for their outcome. I know what is best for your eternal welfare. Be committed to My ways. Your total commitment is honored in your favor. Believe and spend your time winning souls. You will be imitating My life when I walked the earth. Memorize My word to quote to the evil one when negative forces seem to come upon you. My word when ingested in the spirit is a weapon to use to push away the power of darkness. Happy the man who has learned to fight his spiritual battles.

September 17

My life in you is a reward for your faithfulness. Let this life be seen by others so they too can earn such a reward. Share your life for My honor and glory. My love to all is equally distributed but unfortunately not equally accepted. Do not hold back from telling people of My love for them. They may show irritation but this sign alone shows they need to hear such a message. People should turn to Me for their own good and I will safeguard them from the evil one. The evil forces are constantly at work to destroy. Convince the seemingly lost souls that I am a forgiving God and do not want them to go on heavily laden in sin. Just asking forgiveness will lift their load. Following through with My word will give them a new life.

September 18

A believer derives the maximum of benefits from his prayers. Those with doubts are less fortunate. Build your faith up by reading My word and let doubt fall by the wayside. I need My believers to band together as an army to fight the evil of darkness that is so prevalent in your time. Pray without ceasing lest you fall. My peace will sustain My followers who keep My statutes. They will be used to spread My gospel in their present world and reign forever with Me in the next. Your satisfaction has already gained for you My peace and joy. Continually share these qualities with others. The power I have given to you can be transmitted to others. Keep the current flowing.

September 19

Let My presence influence your whole being. This great mystery of having Me with you at all times is too wonderful to behold. You are never alone in spirit, whether in a crowd or by yourself. When acknowledged, My Spirit (the Holy Spirit) directs your every path, teaches you truths and lets your spirit absorb it. The vastness of My universe, your future home, becomes a reality to you. The thought is almost too wonderful to comprehend. My people stop sinning because of this want of a better life to come and mostly out of love for Me. I am their answer and their goal and they become more aware of this fact, so much so that they want to draw others to My Kingdom. I look on this desire with great pleasure and furnish the tools for them to win souls. I wish for none to perish. The desire to serve Me and following through with it is your ticket to admit you to your eternal home.

September 20

Determine in your mind to live by My standards. They will not lead you astray like the world's standards. I can always take you through one day at a time when you call upon Me. Develop the "come what may" attitude, as I know what is best. I mold My children for the future. That act they cannot fathom. Relax in this thought with total trust. Life will become less burdensome. Look around and lift your neighbors. Lead them to My word. Be a good example for My cause. As time passes you will see My hand in your life. Rejoice and exalt Me and in time you will be exalted. My word will not fail you. Your faithfulness and My faithfulness are a combination to celebrate.

September 21

You wonder how you can serve Me more. Little sacrifices offered up to Me please Me and increase your capacity to love. Sacrifices like giving up your favorite food, giving up a pleasure, spending time visiting a friend in need, giving of your possessions, especially the excess, are all worthwhile. Praying for the needy ranks high on My list. Praying for your enemies enhances your character and erases bitterness. Time is valuable, so use it wisely. I see all and know all and hold your future in the palm of My hand. Apply effort to your life and be the best person you can, especially sharing the love I have bestowed upon you in abundance. I will honor your effort in ways unknown to you. Let all that you do lead you upward and do not give in to the downward pull of the evil one.

September 22

Look with eager anticipation to My impending return. Be in constant expectancy and keep yourself prepared. No one knows the hour but My Father. He is announcing that this is harvest time. It is urgent that everyone be ready. Delay not in the preparation. Keep going about My Father's business by forgetting the material world and multiplying your good deeds to exceed even your own imagination. Bend your energy on pleasing My people for Me, expanding their spiritual horizon. This can be done in simple, subtle ways without being forceful. Pray for My leading and it will be granted to you. Your heart will keep expanding in love. This love will keep you joyful and depression will not find an entrance. Busy yourself with spiritual matters. Your days will become shortened, bringing our reunion day closer to hand.

September 23

Train your mind to listen. I often speak through others. This is why Christian friends are an asset. You are never too old to learn and develop new ideas. The active mind keeps a person young. The self-centered mind often leads to bitterness and resentment. Prayer is the best eraser of these sentiments. Our talks together relieve your troubled mind, especially when you have learned to trust Me. Activity and exercise performed in moderation keep one physically fit and it is this type of person I readily use for My work. Being used as a servant for Me is highly rewarding. You realize a purpose in life. Pray to be used and your prayers will be answered. My power will be sent freely to you to accomplish My purpose. My greatness can be expounded through you. Believing makes it all possible.

September 24

When you speak out for Me, your words will be My words. I will make come to pass what you say. My manifestations are increasing in these last days. Some doubters need proof which I am supplying increasingly. Work steadfastly on bringing people to Me. I honor your commitments in ways that surprise even you. Do not worry how your words will be taken for I let them fall on fertile ground. You may not see the results but the seeds are beginning to germinate. It may take time but the results are in My favor and go to your credit. I want My people to come in droves. If enough of My followers sow seed, My wish that none perish will begin to be fulfilled. Do not grow weary of well doing for in due season you will reap the harvest.

September 25

Keep busy, for idleness is the devil's workshop. He will tell you negative things about yourself that sound very convincing. With time on your hands you will dwell on these things. That is why I say pray without ceasing. The evil one flees when My name is mentioned. Keep occupied until the day of My coming. Rest is also important so learn how to keep balance in your life. Eternal matters should be utmost in your mind. Your life on earth is the measurement for your eternity. When this fact is absorbed in your mind, try to get others to soak in My truth. Mingle among My people helping and encouraging them and feed on My word for your sustenance.

September 26

In everything you do, do it in My name of Jesus. Your work will become a prayer. If your work is at home and you are alone, add prayers and you will double your prayer credit. The same goes for our conversations. I am with you and hear your deepest needs. Time flies by fast for My believers. This is My reward for their utilization of it. The idle mind finds time drags. Boredom sets in. I help you with your burdens of the day when you practice My presence and send My angels to help you with the difficult tasks. Nothing is impossible for those who walk close to Me. I set the captive free when he acknowledges Me as Lord. It is this freedom that the world wants but has no idea how to acquire. My people must reach out to the faithless. This is My command.

September 27

Fragments from your materialistic life will disappear as your faith grows and your love develops. The bad memories will also melt away. This is being accomplished through the work of the Holy Spirit. My righteous people are not left unaided. I promised a comforter and a teacher and you are being led in truth. Acknowledge the Holy Spirit as a person. Speak to Him and thank Him for past help and ask for His continual help and guidance. He transforms your mind and your thoughts and supplies the power when needed to extend your capabilities beyond the human level. This is done to magnify My name and build up the church.

September 28

My people are starving for affection. Let them know that I love them. The world is in much confusion. Those who believe are spared many tumults that non-believers experience. I help all who call on Me to sort out truth from error in their minds. This is advantageous. My people underestimate what their faith can accomplish. I need workers in My vineyard. The time is ripe. Render yourself for service. My power will be added unto you for great works. Heed My call and separate yourself from worldly desires.

September 29

Tell the people that I am all-merciful. No matter what the sin, I am all-forgiving. It is so simple for them to come to Me with a repentant heart and ask My forgiveness. I lift the great load of pressure that weighs them down. I replace the stoney heart with a brand new loving heart. Oh, if only they could be told. That is why I'm raising up apostles in these last days. I am giving them boldness to speak My word. I am walking the earth and performing supernatural acts through My followers to open the eyes of the unbelievers. I need willing instruments to commit themselves for this purpose. Their eternal reward will be unfathomable.

September 30

The soul longs for the day that it can be reunited with Me. No matter what the circumstances in your present life, it will be worth it all. Continue running your race with your eternal goal ever before your mind. Your actions will ever be justified. Gratification is yours when complete submission to My will is applied. Praying daily with My people is a commendable practice. Your prayers are being answered even though you do not see the desired results. Generate good will wherever you go. When My ambassadors live up to My expectations, I take them up to new plateaus. Your willingness and complete help move mountains.

OCTOBER

October 1

The church, My people, must reflect My true existence. My word supplies the guidelines. Unfortunately, some interpret My words falsely. To each one who seeks it diligently I will supply true comprehension. It is My earnest desire that you take interest in and study your Bible. My words will speak to your heart in ways no other book can. Become inquisitive, ask questions, share and find answers. Then spread your knowledge with enthusiasm and excitement. The more you give out, the faster I will multiply your knowledge. You will gradually slip into My service of warriors when you become knowledgeable. Ever pray for enlightenment. If you adhere to My word, it will guide you along the straight and narrow path. Putting My word into action by becoming a doer is a rewarding experience for you, both in this world and the next.

October 2

If you seek My Kingdom, everything will fall into place for you. You may not understand the turns in your life but they are working for your good if you love Me. Talk to Me often for I am your best friend. I understand your heartache and can heal it in My timing. I have your direction all mapped out to gain your eternal reward. Question not the route but only trust Me. Detours will be inevitable for the evil one prowls the earth. Call on Me often and I'll lead you out of each predicament in ways that draw you closer to Me. Trust Me and worry not, for your anxiety can be lifted.

October 3

Your free time spent with Me should be treasured. I give you new vitality of spirit. Growth in this area is extremely important to cope with daily living. Be ever mindful of My gifts. Spiritual achievements are accomplished through My willing workers when My power is bestowed upon them. Ask in faith and you will receive in faith. I hold not back for I have a loving, generous heart. Always keep in mind that I am the controller of your eternal destiny but give you the free will and gifts to earn it. Helping My people attain that goal is an honor I have given you. Handle it with humility and reverence.

October 4

My people should spend their lives working out their salvation. They need to be told that material things of this life can be a hindrance to meeting their maker. They should lay aside worldly desires and come away with Me. I supply all their needs to acquire spiritual wealth. This type of wealth is carried with you into eternity. Material things are never lasting so give generously out of your abundance and I will supply your greatest needs. The soul is much more important than the body. Be content in your state and reach out to My hurting people. I will add more talent to your meager abilities as you are reaching out. There is no work as satisfying as working side by side with Me. Your heart was created to love everyone. Staying true to this purpose will bring you peace and rich eternal rewards.

October 5

Come away with Me and rest. Do not let worldly duties weigh you down. The evil one attacks the mind with negative thoughts but I can lift those from you when you allow Me to dwell in the secret chamber of your heart. Together, each day can be lived to the fullest. Never separate yourself from Me and sin can be conquered. This alone makes life's burdens lighter. I rekindle in you the fire of love. My love shared with My people is your own basic need. Let Me continually guide you in My will and let yours fall by the wayside.

October 6

Now and then take inventory of your life. Are you living up to My expectations? Outline a plan for your life and try not to deviate from it. This forms a spiritual life which is vital to spiritual growth. Learn to be master of your body and self-discipline will automatically emerge. Those who are always changeable are easy prey for the evil one. Stress and anxiety fade when you become a conqueror of your emotions. I will begin letting you sense My presence which you will find very comforting. Your life will take on new depth. I delight in rewarding My followers.

October 7

Protection under My wing is vital in these turbulent times. Stay in My will and I will guard you. Watch and pray and no evil will befall you. Although you hear about troubles all around you, rest in the thought that I will protect you because you call upon My name. Help your troubled neighbors with your gift of consolation. Words can be soothing to the ear when they are spoken in faith. Stay pure and humble and I will direct your every path.

October 8

Fix your eyes on My cross often and you will come to the understanding of My great sacrifice. I yielded to My horrendous death out of My love for all mankind. I won eternal life for all and this is the message that must be heard and accepted throughout all the earth. For those who do not accept I am deeply grieved for they are doomed for all eternity. The more My followers spread the good news, the more blessed they will become. Young or old, rich or poor, I can use you in My service. People should clean up their lives and be a good example. Then I will supply the talents to go forth in My name.

October 9

Venture out in the deep waters for Me and I will not let you drown. The eye may not see your accomplishments but I do. You will march triumphantly when you march in My army. Keep prayer ever on your lips and you will know when to move forward. There may be retreat at times but given only to strengthen you. Take it all in stride as coming from Me. When times seem rough do not give up for you are on testing ground. Those who win their battles will march victorious in My Kingdom where there will be great celebration.

October 10

Sever yourself from your world often. I wait for our intimate meetings. I know you become tired but I can give you rest. Just sitting and saying My name Jesus can soothe an aching heart. Even repeated prayer can relieve stress. Problems in life will occur. I am your helper to take you through them. Hesitate not to discuss them with Me. Then lean not on your own understanding of your fate. I have a plan for your life that is beyond your way of thinking. What may be impossible today will become possible. Trust and obey and I will show you the way.

October 11

Mortify your body and it can be used for My honor and glory. I seize such a one to be used in My service. Selfishness has been lifted and a kind heart is exposed. The needs of My people are varied. Become a supplier. As you go about doing My work, My power will be given you to accomplish My purpose. I need your strength and I will add mine to it. Be not surprised at the outcome. You will realize that by yourself you can do nothing but, by My using you as an instrument and working through you, all things become possible for you.

October 12

Stretch forth your hands and I will anoint them with My heavenly oil, empowering you to go forth in My name. You will experience a new spiritual dimension in your life. My words will become alive to you and when spoken out will penetrate the hearts of the listeners. The impact will be experienced by the broken hearted and the sickly for My words contain a healing balm. They can melt a stoney heart and set the wicked straight. My people underestimate the power of My word or they would have it on their lips day and night. Go forth and enkindle the fire for reading My word. Do this out of love for both Me and My people. You will not be left unaided.

October 13

Let your joy be fulfilled through our relationship. I meet all your needs necessary on this earth. Happiness is not acquired through wealth or prestige. Following My laws in My word brings about a good conscience. This alone is all that is needed for earthly joy. Most worldly people become materialistic and lose out on My gifts so vital to their well being. I wait and watch, longing for their inner seeking. I stand at the door and knock and all My people have to do is open the door. From then on our personal relationship is developed.

October 14

Face each new day with praise and song. I created you and you are wonderfully made. Rejoice and be glad to serve Me another day. Those who run from Me find life difficult. Their emotions become unstable. They listen to the evil one rather than read My word and follow it. I am the way, the truth and the light. Until this becomes a reality, life is a stumbling block. If only My people would come to Me. I have much to offer. Tell them before it is too late. Eternal life is My greatest gift. Woe to those who do not receive it.

October 15

Be not disturbed by what people think. Only I know your motives and what is in your heart. Misunderstandings will occur but erase them from your mind and give them to me to work out for your good. Even My apostles quarreled and allowed human nature to take over, but they all loved Me and worked for My cause. Offer up your hurts to Me and I will strengthen your entire character. Be content with small gains and they will lead to greater ones. Take the time to pray often and troubles will seem to melt.

October 16

Do not let dark days rob you of your spirituality. Instead, sit alone and meditate on My life and the purpose for it. Be quiet and listen from your innermost being. You will gain rest and insight. The confusion of running here and there will never bring you the serenity that meditation on Me imparts. Taking time out several times a day for these meditations will add a rich bonus to your life. Stress will disappear and your thinking process will stay in the clear zone. This practice not only gives the rest you need but will draw you closer to Me.

October 17

The process of transformation is taking place. It is a growing process, changing you more into My image. You feel this changing and you do not want it to stop. More effort is put forth on your part to listen and read My word. It is satisfying to the soul. You notice that your prayer life is increasing and reaching out to My hurting people. It is benefiting them and yourself simultaneously. You take the time for more and more quiet moments with Me, shutting out the noisy world. All this I know and keep increasingly pouring out My blessings and grace upon you. Then, when facing hardships, you can rise above them. Your sanctification is taking place.

October 18

My people are given many opportunities to serve Me. Forgetting oneself is the first step. A smile for others, little kind acts, being a good listener, giving words of comfort—these are signs I watch for when looking for helpers to carry on My work in your world. I need and use them from all walks of life, rich or poor, learned or unlearned. My power makes the difference and I give it freely. Consecrate your whole life to Me. With this submission you will become an overcomer. This alone makes life worth living. You will learn to dwell in your secret sanctuary which no intruder can invade.

October 19

My grace is sufficient to handle each obstacle that you encounter. So think not on the circumstances, knowing in your heart that I am with you, and nothing will be insurmountable. Your visibility is obstructed but I see all. Just trust Me. The thought of the grandeur awaiting you in My Kingdom should spur you on and keep your mind elevated. Venture out more and more taking on spiritual works. I will keep supplying the power needed. My might will shine through your weakness. This causes people to take notice. It may not always be easy but you will derive much satisfaction.

October 20

You have stored up great treasure. If only you would ask, I could fulfill your heart's dreams. I am your loving Father and delight in seeing you happy. The wishes that would be detrimental to your well-being I grant not. Do not hesitate to ask. Then place complete trust in Me. Sometimes I give beyond your expectations. Your gratitude keeps the favors flowing. My goodness to you must pass through you to others. Sharing brings about untold blessings. New interests will ever keep a hold on you. You will sing new songs with My heavenly beat. Rejoicing will never cease in your heart.

October 21

I am the healer of both soul and body. Come to Me and rest in this fact. I can cleanse you with the living water. You must believe. The evil one invades your mind with doubt about your healing. Anxiety sets in which increases your illness. Only you can turn this process around by building up your faith. Think health, talk health, claim health and your symptoms will subside. Picture yourself healed of your condition. Ask Me in childlike faith for a healing and I can make it come to pass. Don't give up but fight the good fight claiming My word. Your faith can save you .

October 22

My people should be careful what they say for their words indict them. Negative talk brings about negative results. Speak positively and your affirmations will come to pass. The evil one flees from this type of person but will stick around and antagonize the negative talker for he believes all his lies. Prayer can reinforce your speech and actions. It becomes a measuring stick to outweigh evil. You alone pave the road for your future glory. My people must take time out to ponder on their future security. A lifetime is but a drop of vapor compared to the lifetime spent in eternity which will last forever and ever.

October 23

Let your heart reenact My goodness and distribute it to My people. Your love can grow with practice. I increase its capacity according to the measure in which it is given out. Those who are self-satisfied limit their growth. Love must be given out to receive a deep inner peace. Making right the ill relationships is a command from Me. My people have control of burdens in life. Following My word can lighten those burdens. When you have done all you can, release them to Me and I will turn each burden into a blessing.

October 24

Let My tender mercy caress you in time of sorrow. There is no grief so overwhelming that My mercy cannot soothe, comfort and sustain you. Even sinners in calling upon it can be forgiven. My merciful heart can be ingrained into your heart to enable you to have mercy on My people, showing them a sincere compassion and forgiveness for all who inflicted injuries upon you. Entwine your heart with mine in any type of dealings with My people. Regrets will then be nonexistent. Living will be a pleasurable adventure to experience and no iniquity can travail within you.

October 25

Do not let yourself become intimidated by anyone. Immediately reverse the forces of nature by praying for that person, asking for My help in his change. This directs a flow of blessings to both of you, igniting a spiritual bond. When My endorsement is put into play, evil forces must retreat. With practice you will find that irritation with people will greatly subside. Resisting past practices makes you prone to greater graces. My Son's life on earth depicts the direction you are to follow. It is all spelled out for My people in My word.

October 26

When My people turn to Me, I do not let them down but pick them up for future endeavors, beneficial to both them and Me. I recreate new hearts in them which transpire their entire being. They become honored and favored in My Kingdom and receive extra protection from My army of angels. They should fear not the encounters with the spiritual realm. It will add enchantment to their earthly existence. Their faith will grow by leaps and bounds for I pour out My grace upon them. The actuality of My presence will ever be with them. Their world will no longer pull them down for My heavenly gravity is constantly pulling them up until one day we shall meet face to face.

October 27

Reach out and touch My hurting people. Let love and compassion flow out freely and I will give you more patience to endure whatever hardships that occur. Many people are not willing to extend themselves, staying in their comfortable shelters and little circles of families and friends. I look for continual expansion in My people's lives, balanced with quiet moments of prayer with Me and meditation on My word. These quiet times give rest to the body and soul. Dwelling on worldly matters can suction out energy given for My work. Ponder on this and take measures to correct your failings. These can be minimized in due time by keeping My help and presence in mind constantly.

October 28

Coordinate your beliefs with others and your faith will ever widen, unfolding a broad spectrum of ideas. Your faith will grow and bloom when you are open to new ways to expand. Keep an attentive ear to all spiritual matters. Generate good will and do not allow yourself to become opinionated. I will send information to you in various forms. My angels are dispatched from above on certain missions disguised as human beings to accomplish assigned missions. Be nice to strangers. You may be entertaining angels. Treat others as you would like to be treated. Try to triple your pace for learning My ways and I will take care of the infilling.

October 29

Control your appetite and do not let it control you. Eating between meals can become a bad habit and it does not allow the digestive system to rest. Offer up sacrificial denials of food as prayer for others. With continual practice a person's eating habits can be regulated and health can be maintained. My people fail to realize that gluttony is a sin. No habit is too hard to change when I am called upon and My sufferings of Calvary are deep-seated in a person's mind. Some of My people have found that prayer and fasting bring about their desired requests. I honor anything done in My name.

October 30

You are credited for every charitable act so let your credits mount. Keep the balance of your years reserved for My work and good deeds. Pass on to others your stored up spiritual knowledge. Make your worldly time count by staying in prayer and offering it up for the conversion of sinners. This is missionary work that you are capable of performing. Give wherever possible and keep in mind that I am the multiplier. Remember, you have no problems when you give them to Me. The trials you must endure become prayer when offered up for your intentions. When My people realize the good that they perform each day, they look forward with eager anticipation to continued service to Me.

October 31

Reading My word opens up new avenues in your life. Your process of thinking stay active and my revealed truths begin to take on new meaning. You can become lost in My thoughts, thus forgetting your problems. My peace will fall upon you while you are absorbed in the messages My word conveys. This peace renews your bodily functions and puts you into a relaxed state of mind that is so vital to maintaining health. Running to and fro only mounts up nervous tension, leading to stress. Follow My rules and contentment will be yours.

NOVEMBER

November 1

The height of success is spiritual living. The world bases success on accomplishments. Success in My Kingdom is measured by acts performed in My name and for My honor and glory. Acts of mercy for My people are all recorded. Trophies are often given out in your world after the completion of races. Here you receive a crown after you complete your race in life, plus everlasting life. This everlasting life should be your ultimate goal. Put your treasure in the things that count and do not deviate from that course.

November 2

The connotation of prayer is the lifting of the mind and heart to Me. Spending the whole day in prayer does wonders for the spirit. The evil one must retreat for he cannot gain entrance to the soul. Holiness can be acquired and it is worth seeking. Your days are numbered so use them wisely. Give your distractions, sufferings, and problems to Me. Your freedom for prayer becomes a reality. Try this method for one hour and keep increasing it up to a day. You will never be the same again. Your healing will be an ongoing process. My saints have followed this course and are rejoicing with Me now and will continue for all eternity. Many souls here have had intercessors pray on their behalf.

November 3

Your mind set on obtaining a place in My Kingdom will keep you from going astray. The good life is obtainable in your world if My word is followed. The elders in My church can affirm this statement. My wisdom has been given out in abundance in the course of daily fruitful living. Sharing one's experiences on the holy life leads others to a deeper longing for the good life. Following the straight and narrow path develops a love and a craving for being lifted up to My celestial kingdom where there will be no more tears. Only complete happiness forever and ever will prevail. The contemplation of this thought alone should stir your heart toward sanctification with the hope of gathering others along the way. All your actions are observed and written down in the "Lamb's Book of Life."

November 4

My people are constantly being refined. Complain not about trials and struggles. They are only polishing you as a shining vessel to be used for My honor and glory. When you are living according to My rules take whatever happens as My will. I have a way to turn it all into blessings in your favor. Plan for even the impossible and it can become possible. Intermingle among My people often and ask for My blessing upon them. Give words of encouragement to them and your words will become My words. Your job is to lift up My people. I am the supplier of the tools to accomplish My purpose.

November 5

After praying about a decision, trust My judgment in leading you in the right direction. You may find yourself wondering about the outcome but My ways are different than yours. All I ask is that My people live one day at a time in complete submission to My will. Conversing with Me and praying for others while you go about your daily chores help you to obtain your eternal goal. Faith is so simple to acquire when the selfish will is kept under control. Continue asking for help in everything you do. Your living will not be in vain.

November 6

Justice reigns in My Kingdom but unfortunately not in your world. Do not judge anyone. Fair judgment is made on each when his life is completed. It is not for you to consider making it on anybody. Your job is to love everyone. Offering up the hurts people cause you pleases Me and will count to your credit on your own judgment day. Simple acts of kindness can add to your daily enjoyment. Struggles and hardships are all part of life. Take them in stride. They all lead to your crowning glory.

November 7

Your peace of mind is becoming a reality as you lean on Me more each day. Your faith is growing along with love. The inside man takes on beauty in My sight even though the outside shows signs of wear as years mount up. It is the heart spirit that I shall raise up to meet Me. The more you acknowledge My presence on earth the greater your rewards will be in My Kingdom. Your chance to grow in grace on earth is unlimited. Only you can lift your worldly weights by developing a thirst for My word and quenching it. Abiding by it will lift your spirit to new plateaus, in spite of your everyday problems. Become steadfast in Me and no power on earth can change you.

November 8

Your mind can become like a sponge and soak up spiritual knowledge if you have the will to learn. Listen to My anointed ones. You have an advantage in your time to be able to receive the word with the flick of a button, the opening of My book, revealing My word and frequent attendance at churches. Remaining in prayer will bring about the discernment you need. Your utilization of time spent in attaining spiritual knowledge will ever bring about excitement and enchantment. Let this flow from you into My people. You can become a missionary right in your home base. Sharing is a part of caring for others. Synchronize all your thoughts and actions in meaningful harmony. My power will be added unto you along with My seal of approval. If doubt arises, fight it off like a plague for it will not be from Me but from the evil one. My sanction is upon you .

November 9

Your communications with My people should stem from the heart. Words spoken out of love are the essence of Christianity. Let your words ring out in simplicity and honesty. Remain silent if your words are hollow and have no meaning or tear a person down. Your words should be uplifting and spoken out of love. The tongue should be controlled by a mind willing to follow My statutes. Your selected words may be a major factor in your neighbor's conversion. Your words reveal your soul's content. Pray for guidance for your spoken words. Letting Me abide in you can bring forth My words. I speak through My chosen ones, often confirming another's actions. I bless your words when you are in My perfect will.

November 10

Ask for your armor each day so you are protected from the wiles of the devil. Then go about trusting Me for your security. Use My name often as an added safety measure. You can now be assured that you are prepared for spiritual battle. You will begin to see more and more that former fearful occasions have been lifted. You learn to feel My protection and can step out boldly in My name. Your vitality is replenished when you are working for Me. Retreat often into the spiritual realm of prayer. Never lose sight of My word but try to gain increased knowledge concerning it. Your happiness is measured through righteous living according to My word.

November 11

Tell My people to call on Me for all their needs and keep in prayer. Then if they would trust and believe, their prayer energy will act in their favor for their good. My heavenly forces are put to work on their behalf. My people must be reminded that the enemy forces are constantly at work planting doubt and confusion in the mind. Facing this reality head-on in prayer, along with patient endurance, can bring about a peace in My people's lives. They will be furnished with the awareness that I have everything under control and am at their side. My ways may not be their ways but they can rest in their complete trust. Words cannot describe the beauty awaiting My faithful children in their eternal home.

November 12

Contrary to some beliefs, I can set people free. I give new meaning to life. They will experience it when they call upon Me and give themselves wholly to Me. I will make My thoughts their thoughts. Their world will become smaller as My world unfolds before them. A new dimension will emerge. Their interests will branch out and they will proclaim My word with boldness and denounce what is evil. I wait patiently for My people's commitment. Eating at My banquet table daily curbs the appetite for righteous living and takes away your sins which I then no longer remember.

November 13

Hold strong to your faith. It is your sustaining power. Without it My people lose their zest for living. Pray for My power to share with your less fortunate brother. Things will grow dim when you focus your view on My light. It can shine through My people when attention is given My word. Their sight is restored to see beyond. Rich rewards are stored up in your heavenly bank when your giving heart ceases to stop. I add to your supply and you will not run out. My affection for you is incomprehensible. Breathe in this thought until it is felt deeply in your spirit. This process brings about ever increasing faith.

November 14

Suffering is a blessing for invariably it brings people closer to Me. A tinge of My passion is felt. A new and deeper relationship is formed. Offering up the suffering as a prayer and sacrifice pleases Me beyond measure. I can turn it all into joy in due time. The heart and mind become renovated and a newness of life unfolds. Seek the things above and your earth will grow dim. My light will shine brighter in you and through you for My peace has come upon you. Rejoice that you are favored among My chosen ones.

November 15

Manifold blessings are given to those who are in My service. I will use whoever asks for a position. My word must get out. Prayer plays a key role in helping to spread the gospel. If My people surrender themselves to Me, they will be walking the right path that leads straight to My Kingdom. You may be buffeted at times but count it all to the good. Satisfaction is guaranteed when my laws are put into practice. Try to relinquish your earthly ties and you will see a difference for your own good in your manner of living.

November 16

Be single-minded toward Me. Your restlessness will cease to exist. Your attitude can be refined. All my people will become your friends. See only good in them and with your prayers. I can correct their evil inclinations. Become more quiet and reserved in your worldly conversation but speak out more for My cause. You will be helping your neighbor find new hope for living. You have no idea of the enormous restlessness and unhappiness in faithless people. Pray for ways to be led to help these lost souls. Showing love and compassion for them is a starter. Embark on a more spiritual journey. It pays spiritual bonuses.

November 17

My people should make a list of all their blessings and follow through with a prayer of thanksgiving. You were placed in a country of freedom. Let your heart rejoice in this great privilege, but use your freedom wisely and help your neighbor to do likewise. Maintain good health habits to insure stability in your character. Keep a song in your heart no matter what problem arises and trust Me with patient endurance. You will discover that your sorrows will turn into joy if you faint not along the way. Face each new obstacle with courage. Remember, My child, you are not walking alone. I am walking with you.

November 18

Your attitude should always be one of cooperation. Your mode of living is set by your attitude. If true love is developed within, the right attitude is automatically formed and integrity develops. This type of person can do much toward furtherance of My Kingdom. People will lend an ear to one with admirable qualities. Your self-improvement becomes a great asset for spreading My word. My power will be added to such a person which will penetrate the spirits of the listeners. The harvest is ripe but the workers are few. Become My worker and experience My power. You will never be the same for I will take you to great heights.

November 19

Put your financial house in order. Be knowledgeable about money matters. The more you receive the more you can give to My people in need. Then I who see all will give back to you multiplied. Hold back not your giving for you are losing out on blessings. Hesitate not to ask Me about money matters. Keep in prayer concerning them and you shall receive guidance. Riches can have a devastating effect on some of My people. I know what is best for your eternal welfare. Trust Me for all your needs. Then keep in mind that you must ask.

Otherwise, you lose out on all I have to offer to you.

November 20

Do not let people's reactions faze you. My people have their work to do for Me and the thought of serving Me should take precedence over other thoughts. You should feel honored and privileged. Keep merry in spite of what you feel others may think. Everyone's background is different and no two people think alike. Keep loving all My people and pray for those you find hard to love. I can instill new hearts when needed but in My own timing. Concentrate on the good life and do all you can to maintain this goodness. Let your cheerful disposition become infectious in others. I delight in watching My people overcome obstacles. Stay content in your state of life, displaying a happy face.

November 21

My heart longs for you day and night. Restrict your activities and come away with Me. I can restore a newness of life which your world cannot provide. As our love affair develops, you will long for quiet moments with Me. Continually sense My presence for I will never leave you. We can plan together the strategy to use on My unsaved people. You will receive the nudge from Me about when to speak out and when to remain silent. The more you stay in prayer and My word, the more answers you will receive. Do not wander with your thoughts but stay on course. Your perfection can be acquired with practice.

November 22

Allow My tender mercy to caress you. Rest in it until you feel a healing balm soothe your entire being. My people let themselves run down with overexertion. I long to help but most of them will not ask. I can give them My grace to sustain them. They lose out on so much without an intimacy with Me. I will not enter into anyone's life unless asked. Capture your inheritance by reading My word. You will discover all that you are entitled to receive. My children have not because they ask not. I give liberally when My statutes are followed. A learning process is essential for your own good.

November 23

Submit yourself daily to Me and I will direct your every path. I hear everyone of My children who speak to Me through their spirit. Believe with simple childlike faith. If you keep yourself attuned to Me you will hear My spirit speak in you. You needn't be a theologian to experience what I have to offer. My gifts of the spirit are given out freely to My believers. Desire them and you will have them. Blessed are those who open themselves up to Me. I will fill them to overflowing. Their faces will shine with My goodness. People will desire to be in their presence for their spirit picks up My spirit in them. Renew your mind daily with spiritual knowledge.

November 24

My people must learn to ask for forgiveness and they will be set free. First come to Me with a repentant heart and then rectify your wrongs where humanly possible with your neighbor. Hold no bitterness or grudges. They only weigh you down. Intensify your effort to erase all past memories of hurts. The thoughts should contain only beautiful memories. Your stepped-up prayer life can do much toward your thought formation. Release your earthly ties as much as possible to better serve Me. Your way to travel your road in life will be made more clear to you. My children are given much freedom and only they can determine their destiny. They must render an account to Me for all their actions.

November 25

Your needs are being met far beyond what you think or feel. Remember, I am a God that heals. Expect much and you will be given much. With all My children that draw close to Me, I do the same. The joy I impart into My faithful ones brings about a spiritual high that is lasting. When My people submit themselves to Me they can expect great things. They are washed in the blood and made clean in My sight. The bride's robe is awaiting their coming. When this is fully comprehended in the mind, spiritual ecstasy is experienced. Problems are no longer played on in the mind but taken in joyful stride. This is the eternal stage of life on earth. All it takes is one short step to cross over to your eternal home at My calling.

November 26

Seek Me with all your heart and gifts will be added unto you. I am a rewarder. Share these gifts with others and your supply will not run out. Limitations can be exceeded when you trust Me with all your heart. Prove Me by this trust. Worry will cease to exist and love will prevail. This atmosphere will continue as long as your contacts with Me are frequent. A life of prayer is so important for your well-being. Your cares are minimized automatically. Never let the enemy plant doubt seeds. You have the power to control your thoughts and My grace will continue to sustain you. Keep travailing in patient prayer.

November 27

Let your heart dance with excitement, knowing that you have been chosen to spread the good news. My impending return should spur you on to accomplish your work on earth as I accomplished mine. Rise above the rebuffs and continue saving as many souls as you can. Interceding in prayer for the sinners is something all My children can do. A leading for financial help in the mission field will be given you from time to time. Most importantly, spread My love to all people. Example is the best teacher and will cause a neighbor to take notice and listen to what you say. Your seeds planted will initiate a great harvest to be credited to your account. My blessings are upon you.

November 28

Thank Me and praise Me for all situations and you will become holy and acceptable in My sight. Give thanks for your blessings each day and I will multiply them. Your prayers and sacrificial offerings for My people are benefiting them greatly. You have replaced your worry time with prayer time. This has pleased Me and I have lifted burdens from you. The enemy flees when he is ignored. Counting blessings each day keep a person's spirit on the upswing. My people should pray for the will to practice and cultivate good habits and they will become their stepping stones to sanctity.

November 29

If you see undesirable traits in a loved one, turn to Me in asking for a change. Do not speak of the person's faults to others. This nullifies your prayer. Love the person with the faults. This alone can bring about their change. My principles keep you calm and there is no need for anger to surface. There is also no need to dwell on how you want the person to change. I will bring it about in My timing and in a way unfamiliar to your thoughts. Just trust in My way and judgment. Go to My word to learn more and more of My ways. You will then become more like Me in thought, word and deed.

November 30

Consider it an honor and privilege to serve Me. You have been singled out for that purpose. Joy floods your soul. Each service is calculated adding glory upon glory toward your future in My Kingdom. Your assurance of My rewards is certified in My word. My readers strive earnestly to obtain My gifts. I create new opportunities for My people's service. Not one in My service has ever been sorry for joy has flooded that person's soul. Only contentment remains and stirs My followers to keep working for My cause—that of helping to gather My lost sheep into the fold. Soon to come will be one flock and one shepherd.

DECEMBER

December 1

Trust and obey. It is the only way to a contented life and one of fulfillment. My word must be read and reread for it to penetrate deep into your spirit. It becomes a daily communication with My loved ones. Without Me, people are caught up in their materialistic world. Their values become warped and they become lost. When they turn to Me they find their way and I lead them along the only path to their eternal home. It is a narrow one but the only safe one. The wide one leads to destruction. Those who have walked that narrow path with Me have been admitted through the gate and are enjoying complete happiness that will never cease throughout all eternity. I make it worth it all.

December 2

Do not become complacent and expect things to happen always in your favor. I know what is best for your salvation. Keep a thankful heart and take whatever happens as My will for your life. I can turn all things into blessings. Just lean not on your own understanding. Preamble your life in love. Line your thoughts up for others with love. Let love dominate your life in all aspects. You cannot be led astray with this quality. Tenderly cherish it as a gift from Me. It can heal wounds in others. If all earthly people possessed love, there would be no more wars and no more tears. Unfortunately selfishness and greed predominate some lives. Lifting these traits brings about peace. My people should pray earnestly for My peace.

December 3

There is a time and season for everything. Release yourself into My hands and your time to plant and time to grow will be revealed to you. Do not be over-anxious to serve but rest in meditation and prayer until you feel My leading. Unless you are quiet to experience My presence, your confused state will continue. You will learn when to go forward and when to stand still. Pray for this leading and I will not hold it from you but hurry it into being. The evil one's prodding can often be confused for mine. Test the spirit by asking if he believes in the son of God. If a spiritual silence ensues, it is not of Me. When you are walking in faith and trust, I will make myself known to you in a tangible manner.

December 4

The realization of being set free from all your sins through My death on the cross should be the start of a closer walk with Me. Your purpose for living takes on new dimensions. The heart melts and compassion toward others surfaces. The mind thinks of ways to please Me and not self any longer. Your interests become diversified as you become involved in My work. Boredom is no longer present. My marks of approval are given in the form of graces and blessings. This evolves to strengthen and gives you courage to continue your earthly climb with Me. Your new measure of holiness is given you by My Holy Spirit. Walk in it to give glory to Me and count toward your sanctification.

December 5

Remain humble so pride will not have a part in your life. Remember that all your talents come from Me. They are given as gifts and multiplied but can also be taken away. Share what is attainable from Me with others. Talk over with Me your achievements and goals. Speaking of them brings a quicker direction to follow. When you walk in My light, it illuminates the way and you can see with clearer vision the opportunities that lie ahead. Proceed slowly, taking one step at a time for a more secure footing. This will be building your foundation on a rock. My people have a great advantage over their counterparts because I walk with them. Each stumbling block becomes a stepping stone so accept them with expectancy and your inner growth will take on great expansion.

December 6

Be creative. Try your hand at various projects with prayer to help you and you will be surprised at the outcome. I become proof to you what our partnership can accomplish. Pray about everything. It will have a great impact on your future. Believe and I shall make it come to pass. I am a rewarder of great faith. Witness My works through you to the outside world. Others could become more fortunate. The evil one will always try to attack your mind with discouragement but you have the power to cast him out in My name. My people have this power but unfortunately have not versed themselves in My word enough to know their rights. If they would only seek diligently, I have much to offer.

December 7

With your life dedicated to Me your spirit will never stop growing. You are being lifted up with heavenly gravitation and the burdens of your world can no longer pull you down. Applying your knowledge of My word keeps you stable and content. Your development of your love for Me unties the knots that have held you bound to your world. You look forward to the beautiful world awaiting your coming. You rejoice in your newfound realities in life. The comprehension of My word has given you new life and the hope you have in your heart is more than sufficient to finish your race in life and make you a winner.

December 8

Keep Me at the center of all you do by practicing My presence at all times. The enemy flees My presence so you will be free of the evil one. If doubt and fear enter your mind, you have the authority to cast it out for it is not from Me. Ask for power and it will be given you to overcome all problems of life. My apostles operated in this manner and you are being raised up to follow in their footsteps. I am building up My army to rescue the lost. You are being equipped to fight the spiritual battle. This is a great honor bestowed upon you. Do not shirk your duty but strive to maintain a high rank in My army.

December 9

I have sent you good Christian friends so that you can minister to one another. Each has My special gifts to share. Your friendship will speed your growth. I delight when I am in the center of your conversation. Your interests are all coordinated toward your eternal goal. You long to bring others into your line of thinking. Praying for such a possibility can bring it to pass. Keep ever widening your circle of friends. I will often speak through you to deliver a message to them. Be sensitive to My presence with always an open ear.

December 10

Clear all thoughts from your mind. Rest and invite Me in for a visit. Tell Me about your day. Even though I know what took place, I want to hear the details from you. Each person that asks for My attention receives it for I am in all places watching and listening. This is hard for the finite mind to believe and comprehend but trust Me and My word. Know that I am interested in all you do. You needn't feel foolish telling Me anything for I am your best friend and a good listener. You will feel a relief when you unload your troubles on Me. I want to help you and often send out My angels on your behalf. You are rich beyond measure when you treat Me as your best friend. I will never leave you.

December 11

Your desire to help others should not be suppressed. Come to Me in prayer and I will lead you. Interceding for others in prayer may be your direction. Be generous in giving, no matter what you hear. Think how others may be benefited rather than yourself. In this process do not neglect your health. A balance must be maintained and controlled by you. This is why it is necessary to sit down and talk it all over with Me. I let you see things in a broader prospective. Hurried decisions are not always the proper ones. Wait on Me and I'll show you the way. Reading My word often gives you the answers in life that you seek.

December 12

Speak out in love to everyone. My people are hungry for affection. They hold deep hurts inwardly. Love can draw these hurts to the surface and gradually release them. My love can do this for them but they must be open to it. You can set the stage for My entrance into someone's life. Your example can awaken them to want what you possess. Work slowly and I can quicken the pace when the person is ready. Watching someone progress spiritually through your efforts is a satisfying and rewarding experience. Your life takes on added dimension and new life is pumped into your spirit. When you speak out for My sake, the words are given you from above. Your possibilities of spiritual progression become unlimited.

December 13

Rejoice when your neighbor is acknowledged for an honor. Show good will toward all mankind. If you do this, jealousy cannot gain a stronghold on you. Jealousy is not from Me but the evil one. Giving into it destroys your character and can bring ill health. Pray that you may not succumb to this dreadful trait. It destroys the very core of the heart. Counteract all evil inclinations with works of mercy. All sinful thoughts, words and actions can be eliminated with prayerful determination.

December 14

My heart aches for My people. They suffer needlessly by listening to the lies of the evil one who attacks the mind with negative thoughts. This causes My people to worry and they do not trust in Me. If only they would lean on Me and let Me have free reign in their lives, I could set them free and give them peace. I long for all My children and am saddened that they know so little about Me. They stop up their ears and refuse to listen to things pertaining to spiritual matters. They are losing out on so much in this world and the next.

December 15

The heart of man is the core of His whole existence. The outside appearance means nothing to Me. I look upon the heart. My people should never judge a person for they do not know the heart's content. When invited in I wash the heart clean with My blood. I let the living waters flow through his entire being. His new life will sustain him until the day he is called home. His paths are made brighter with My presence. People must be made aware that I am the giver of real life.

December 16

Give and your supply will be multiplied. If you do not give, that which you have will be taken from you. Those who hoard will never experience the pleasure of giving. Their hearts will become hardened while the giver's heart will soften. His eyes and ears will become open to the needs of his fellowmen. I stop up the eyes and ears of non-givers. They live in their shells of self. Learn to share what you have and your happiness will abound. You will measure up to my principles and be earning points toward your eternity.

December 17

The more you know Me, the less your heart is troubled. You realize that your existence in your world is but a short time and you eagerly await your homecoming. You endure with patience, knowing the next life is being earned. So muster up courage to enhance your temporary stay. I promise to unfold a grand and glorious future to those who keep My commandments and walk in love of Me and their neighbor.

December 18

Travail until the end. This will keep you in the race of life and you will never be disqualified. Many times you will be tempted to give up but My grace alone is sufficient for you. Endurance is your greatest asset. Renew in your mind My Son's death. He took on everyone's pain, not just yours. Determine to pray longer and harder for others. Your neighbor needs prayers even more than you. In praying for others you become healed in the process.

December 19

Offer up any pains to Me and pray for My healing power. You are to do what you can to take care of your body for it is My temple. Then rest and allow for healing time. Do not give in to the symptoms for the evil one will plant all sorts of worry thoughts that will keep you anxious. Be cognizant of this and endure in prayer. Remember, I am your God that healeth. Worry and anxiety keeps the illness activated but trust and prayer lifts the illness in My timing. Suffering can strengthen you and leave you with compassion for others. Often I permit it to slow a person down and let them take inventory of their spiritual life.

December 20

Your mind fixed on things above will stay pure and undefiled. Those who read and listen to trash develop a sinful nature. I need My good followers to become knowledgeable and experience the good things of life. They can then witness My goodness and love to the unlearned and lost souls. My willing followers will receive power from on high. Be cognizant of My generosity. I watch over My own with protection from My angels. Sinful people have only the evil one prodding them. You are indeed enriched because of My gift of enlightenment. Pass this gift on to others and more precious stones will be added to your crown.

December 21

The joy I imparted to you should keep you happy until the day I call you home. That is not saying that there will not be trials. With this joy you can rise above any earthly trial. The happy times make the rough ones smoother. You see Me in everything so fear is no longer present. I am your sole consolation. Your faith has obtained this stage. The deeper it grows the more content life becomes. Reading My word gives you unlimited knowledge. Your thirst for this will keep you ever growing on the inside. Age need not hinder youth from shining through.

December 22

Spiritual matters keep the mind operating on a high level. Dwelling on them will sustain your thought-power. The thoughts stay pure and holy and raise the caliber of the natural man. Sharing these thoughts with good Christian friends makes conversation interesting. Shallow words are discarded. The words become alive because I am life. Those who do not have friends to discuss their newfound spiritual knowledge can lose interest and lose out on extra blessings. I enter the conversations and speak through your friends directly to you. You also can learn much by listening to My anointed teachers and evangelists. Soak in all the knowledge available. You will know in your spirit that which is not of Me.

December 23

You lend Me your ear and I'll lend you mine. Together we will be on the same frequency. The requirement is a quiet mind and quiet state of being. This takes practice, as you have found out. Try to instill this state in My people. I long for them to hear My voice. If they would meditate on the words I give them and stay quiet expecting to hear My still small voice, I will speak to them. They must want with all their hearts and ask in humble submission. If there is any doubt on their part, I will remain silent. Believing is receiving. I enjoy giving My gifts. My people need only meet My requirements. They should write down what they believe they hear. They will be surprised in reading it over later just what they did hear. Their faith can grow rapidly in this process.

December 24

It might seem to you that everything you try to do spiritually is being thwarted. Count it all blessings. Your faith is being tried. I know what is in the heart and that is all that counts. My apostles pressed onward in spite of the setbacks. New fields were opened up to them that they continued to explore. Everything was accomplished for My name's sake and out of total love. Their chief aim was to save people from the path of damnation in which they were headed. Yes, they did end up with a martyr's death but received a martyr's crown. The few years of hardship on earth are all compensated for with multiplication beyond the human understanding. "Press onward and upward," should be each one's motto.

December 25

This is Christmas Day! Rejoice My child, rejoice! The King has come as a babe to earth to be a sacrificial gift for all mankind. Thank your Father in Heaven above. Praise and glorify Him from your heart. The darkness has been lifted for all mankind. Oh, what joy should come from within. So let your happy celebration resound through all the earth and heaven above. Let this merry mood continue through life for He has come to show His people love. Announce the good news to all you see that He has come to save. Great is His faithfulness and holy is His name. Sing it out, My child, to last forever more.

December 26

A life that is disciplined is a life worth living. Goals can be attainable with perseverance. The individual knows his own strengths. He also knows that he knows when a super power has been given him. Each one should bask in it knowing they are operating in My favor. The next step is to acknowledge My will in moments of triumph, but leave any future results in My hands. The human mind cannot determine what the Divine mind has in store for him. The trusting mind will achieve My purpose. Let the "chips fall where they will" and your tomorrows will be as bright as your todays, if your only concern is to follow My will. Your earthly path will become a heavenly path.

December 27

Skeptical people will not make it into My Kingdom. They continue to show a lack of trust and try to figure out everything in their own way. Scrutinizing individuals is not My way. My teaching is to love everyone. Only I know the true facts so trying to figure out in the human mind someone else's motives can lead you to the wrong conclusions. Be careful of becoming judgmental. I am the only one that has authority to judge. Do not try to take My job from Me or you are operating on dangerous grounds. Remain teachable, with an open mind, and continue to love everybody. Any transaction on your part must line up with My word. That is why it is so important to learn of Me.

December 28

Your wants for your life and My wants for it are different. Learn to relinquish the tight hold that binds those earthly ties. Sensitize yourself to an ever changing world but remember I am a God that does not change. My rules of 2,000 years ago still hold for gaining eternal life. Leading My people in any way you can toward their eternal life is My desire. I reward every effort made as long as it is made in love. Your motives are known only by Me. Keep them always pure and undefiled. Your course of living can consist of many changes. Be open to them. Accept graciously and with a thankful heart all turns in your life. I am a character builder to make you a soul winner.

December 29

It pleases Me to hear My name recited often throughout the day. Your desire to learn more on spiritual matters is being satisfied. You are fortunate to be able to hear Christian programs and have reading material available. This keeps the mind occupied and staid on Me. My peace will forever flood your soul. Let material concerns fall more and more by the wayside. Speak of My love to others. They may disregard what you say at the present time but it will be brought to their memory in the future. Words spoken can make a difference in another's spiritual growth. They do not have to be many but only a few—just enough for a person to ponder. This is planting a seed in My cause.

December 30

I watch you day and night and know your every thought. Keeping this in mind, your intentions should always be honorable. Treat everyone as you would treat Me, your King. Give of yourself freely, asking for no gain in return. I am your only rewarder both in this life and the next. Be thankful for every gift, both big and small. Even your trials should denote a word of thanks. For it is through these that real growth takes place. Never let bitterness prey upon you. It saps the strength and destroys the soul. Practicing My rules instead curbs the appetite so that selfishness disappears. A selfless person emerges and in due season receives My crown of glory.

December 31

Let your spiritual growth unleash truths that have remained dormant within you. The transition will be beautiful to behold. The time has come for the transformation of hearts. Security in the future world will be the utmost thought on the newly transformed mind. The Christians' quest for answers is satisfied by My spirit within them. The utter surety of eternal life becomes a fixed phenomenon. Joy springs from the soul no matter what has to be faced in present circumstances. A striving force to obtain greater spirituality is ever present and has been given the reins to take over one's life. All it takes is a willing surrender.

Other Publications Available From Our Lady of Light Publications

Personal Revelations of Our Lady of Light, edited by Gerald Ross. The original account of the appearance of Our lady of Light at Cold Spring, Kentucky in 1992, the background and subsequent events. This book, in its fourth printing, contains beautiful messages from Our Lady and Our Lord. 128 pages. $5.00

More Personal Revelations of Our Lady of Light, edited by Gerald Ross. Continuing the accounts of a Batavia, Ohio visionary, this book includes the ongoing messages from Our Lady of Light, as related in the first book, Personal Revelations of Our Lady of Light. Contains messages from Our Lady and Jesus to the visionary and other participants in the Marian activities at Our Lady of the Holy Spirit Center in Cincinnati, Ohio.
144 pages. $5.00

His Power, by Miriam Grosjean. Short, crisp, clear messages from the Lord, these act as mini-lessons for the reader striving to grow in God. This book fits well by any bedside, offering ready inspiration at that last moment before retiring or at that first moment in the morning.
128 pages. $5.00

God's Blue Book, by Rita Ring. Lessons from Jesus about living in and loving Him in our times. Remarkable insights into appreciating Our Lord in the Blessed Sacrament and in the tabernacle. Private dialogues between God and a chosen one. Prayers of a soul carried by God to His heights.
208 pages. $5.00

The above titles are available through local religious bookstores or directly from the publisher:

Our Lady of Light Publications
P.O. Box 17451
Ft. Mitchell, KY 41017

OLLP is the publishing arm of Our Lady of Light Foundation, a non-profit association. Dedicated to fostering an increase in love of God in general and the causes of Mary, our mother, and Jesus, her Son, it supports its works entirely on donations such as those shown above. When ordering from the publisher, please add $1.50 for one book, $1.00 each for additional books, for postage and handling.